Let This Cup Pass

Let This Cup Pass

Jane McWhorter

QUALITY PUBLICATIONS

P.O. BOX 1060   ABILENE, TEXAS 79604

ISBN: 0-89137-414-0

Weeping may endure for a night,
But joy cometh in the morning.

—Psalms 30:5

ACKNOWLEDGEMENTS

I would especially like to express my gratitude to the ladies' Bible class at Fayette, Alabama, for their comments and suggestions in the initial study of this material.

Gibson Greeting Cards, Inc. for permission to use three poems by Helen Steiner Rice:
"Before You Can Dry Another's Tears"
"Climb 'Til Your Dreams Come True"
"The End of the Road is But a Bend in the Road"

Cover design by Craig Webb

Chapter titles by Foy Bobo

TABLE OF CONTENTS

The following article, written by my husband, appeared on February 3, 1972 in the **Gospel Advocate.**

WHY?

"Why?" is the most timeless and universal of all questions, as old as the first tear and as recent as the latest newscast. The answer to that complex and baffling question is in the Word of God, and that is one of the many reasons that Book is both timeless and universal. Why must there be suffering, sorrow, heartache, death, even among God's own children? With the recent death of a dear father and the tragic automobile accident that injured my entire family, Jane so critically, I have thought about this question many times. When the accident occurred we were on our way to our former home in Gadsden, Alabama to assist a dear friend in laying to rest the body of his mother, a Christian lady as close to Jane and me as our own family. We were driving slowly and carefully and yet someone took our lane and hit us head-on in a car traveling much too fast. Though I was insured in case I should be guilty of injuring someone else, she had no insurance, not even a driver's license. Two members of my family were nearly killed and it will require at least a year for the recovery of Jane's health. The head injury alone resulted in the fracturing of her skull in more than 200 places. Her arm, ribs, back, pelvis, and leg were broken. While we kept vigil in the waiting room of the Intensive Care Unit of Erlanger Hospital for more than a month as her life hung in the balance there was ample time to wonder "Why?" And to the Word of God we continually went. May I share with you some of the conclusions reached?

1. *Suffering keeps this world from becoming too attractive.* Though our dwelling places here may have more permanent foundations than the Bedouin tents of our father Abraham, we are reminded that we are no less pilgrims and strangers. (1 Peter 2:11.) Woe to the man or woman whose life here on this earth is so pleasant that he forgets about heaven. But the affairs of this life are so ordered that this world soon loses its attraction. Most young people would like to live forever but by the time a man reaches his three score and ten he is usually happy he has been able to endure one life and is ready for something better.

This world is too full of pain, grief, and heartache to be very pleasant or attractive for very long.

2. *Suffering brings out our best.* The common bond shared by families in the waiting room welded them into one concerned group. All lost many hours of sleep, all were uncomfortable, all were deeply concerned with their own problems and yet each was deeply aware of the other's needs and did everything possible to make it easier for the others. At times I thought I could feel better if I could muster some hard feelings toward the ones who brought this suffering upon my family. Probably under less trying circumstances these feelings could have come all too easily and yet as I searched my heart here I honestly could find no ill will. Suffering brings out our best. Jane has always been a brave and courageous woman. During this illness she has exhibited a remarkable courage, one that the doctors feel contributed immeasurably to her recovery. That ready smile was always there and since she has been able to talk a word of thanks and praise for all who have ministered to her.

And the best has been brought out in so many others who have shared this burden for us. For a month, twenty-four hours each day, there was always some dear friend in the waiting room to give me a chance to get some rest and to keep me company during those long, lonely hours. For a month breakfast was the only meal that had to be prepared at our house. Food was prepared and brought by the house each day by those who love us. While I didn't get to be home for many of these meals my mother and children, and on occasion, Jane's mother and father, thoroughly enjoyed them. During the week the entire family was hospitalized someone kept the children company in their rooms every day.

So many have been anxious to help share the tremendous expense I have incurred in all this. The hospital bill alone will exceed $10,000. And then there are twelve doctors to be paid. Regardless of the expense they earned every cent and I gladly shoulder that debt. Many individuals and congregations are helping and I know the Lord will provide a way.

Intellectually you know this is the way Christianity works and yet an experience like this serves to deepen the faith of all involved. Jane and I will never be the same and the fine congregation at Greens Lake Road has grown spiritually through this episode in a way they could never have grown otherwise. It has all been for the good.

3. *Suffering gives an occasion to put to silence the enemies of God.* We are all familiar with the sufferings of Job and the eventual outcome of his tribulation. That same experience, in one degree or another, has been re-enacted since the dawn of time. The lady who hit us is hospitalized in the same hospital where Jane is being treated. Christians have visited her, and we have all prayed for her and continually reassured her no one was angry or held any ill will toward her. She is amazed. Others have been amazed at the volume of friends always at the hospital, many driving more than one hundred miles to visit us often. One special incident deserves attention. Jane has a problem that made necessary the availability of fresh blood for transfusions rather than blood stored in the blood bank. During one particular crisis blood was urgently needed and the blood bank was assured that we would have the necessary donors there shortly. They were skeptical and openly so when they learned we were depending on a call through members of the church to find and supply the blood. Within thirty-five minutes of the time the emergency call went out some sixteen members of the church with Jane's blood type were at the hospital ready to supply her need. Even this incident caused others to see the Lord's people in a different light. There is more than one way to silence the enemies of God.

4. *Suffering make us appreciative.* We all receive so many good things that we are prone to take them for granted rather than receive them with gratitude. Through all this many of us have become more aware of blessings we overlook and more thankful for them. How can I ever thank God enough for his goodness? How can I ever show my appreciation to my brethren for their display of love and kindness?

5. *Suffering makes us depend on God.* (Isaiah 54:5.) It is good for a man to come to the realization that it all depends on God (it always does; we just don't always realize it) and to throw himself completely upon his mercy. When a dozen of the most skilled men in their profession tell you they have done all they can and it is completely out of their hands you suddenly realize how much you depend on God. And this awakens your sense of dependency in every other realm as well.

6. *Suffering purifies us.* Peter and James bear testimony to this fact. (1 Peter 4:11, 12; James 1.) Many times I searched my own life during these past six weeks in order to confess my every failure and shortcoming to God. I surely did not want my own sins to stand in the way of God's hearing my prayers for Jane. It was absolutely necessary to be truthful with God and myself and I am a better man today than before.

7. *Suffering makes us sympathetic.* Paul so instructs the church at Corinth. (2 Corinthians 1:3-6.) We may think we sympathize with someone but until we have been there personally there is no real way to sympathize. I am going to spend more time with the sick and it will be because I am better equipped to do a service God expects of the Christian.

8. *Suffering makes one humble.* As I look back at all God has done and continually does how could I help but be humble? As I contemplate what my brethren have done and are doing I am not only thankful and humble but also ashamed. So much has been done for me that I honestly blush to face my Christian friends.

9. *Suffering teaches us how to pray.* I have been a praying man since I became a Christian. But never like this. I have learned more about prayer in the past six weeks than in the previous twenty years. My prayers will be different for the rest of my life. During those dark days when the doctors despaired for Jane's life prayer was going up to God on her behalf from thousands of different lips all over the world. If you run into anyone who does not believe in the power of prayer send him to me; I would like to talk to him. Don McWhorter.

INTRODUCTION

This book is more than just a suitable subject for a Bible class; it is the study of a soul searching for an answer.

The seeds were planted in my mind a number of years ago when my mother was stricken with a painful and deforming malady, rheumatoid arthritis. It is to her memory that this work is dedicated in appreciation for all her love and what she has meant to me. It is with special gratitude to my daddy that I thank him for his untiring care of Mother. Although her body became confined to a wheelchair, her spirit was not; she was an inspiration to all. In spite of her cheerful attitude, there were times when she confided to me that she couldn't understand why this had happened to her. Not knowing the answer myself, I felt my utter helplessness as I watched her body gradually become twisted and deformed. Even though I did not have the solution, my healthy body, which had never known pain, could easily give advice. Several years ago, along with numerous other injuries to my back and limbs, my face was crushed into over two hundred fractures in a head-on collision when a driver in the on-coming lane of traffic lost control of her car. Then it became **my** turn to wonder **why**. It was then that I learned it is much easier to give advice than it is to take it. It was not until that time that I learned how years of constant pain can eat into the very core of one's being. It was then that I began to understand how physical deformities can make one want to run and hide, hoping he would be remembered the way he used to be.

Answers are not always imminent. One phase of the eternally asked question which had now become mine was not answered for several years. As grateful as I had been to have my life spared and a new face reconstructed by the hands of a plastic surgeon, I must confess that there were many times when I shed tears as I longed for my previous face; but I reasoned that I had been given a totally undeserved present—life itself—and should not complain just because it had not been gift-wrapped. This part of my question was not answered until one day four years later when I took a little gift to an elderly woman in a nursing home. With gratitude in her eyes, she looked up at me and said, "You're so pretty." I believe it was at that moment that my heart accepted what I had known for years: true beauty has nothing to do with outward appearance but radiates from within as we lose ourselves in service to others.

The lesson has been a difficult one for me to learn. My mother passed away several years ago, and since then I have grown a little older and much wiser. How I wish I could now sit down with her and try to answer her question. But I can't. I will have to admit that there have been periods of resentment and the shedding of many tears, but time has a way of mellowing the hues and developing a sense of perspective. Now I can see that what happened to me has been one of the greatest blessings of my life because it has made me better on the inside and has drawn me closer to God.

Much as a mother shelters her unborn child within the warmth of her own body, so have I carried the seed of this work within me for a number of years. Like the embryo, who receives his food and oxygen through the bloodstream of his mother, so has **this** seed been nourished through my searching the Scriptures and by many outside sources which I have absorbed into my being as I have sought the answer to my own perplexing question. As the fetus slowly assumes a recognizable form, so has this seed gradually taken shape within me. There have been many times when I have awakened in the stillness of the night, struggled with plausible solutions to the problem, and have then cried myself back to sleep. Now the time has come when I feel that the seed has developed sufficiently to leave my mind and exist apart from me. To you the reader I offer this fruit of my heart. It is delivered with the prayer that it will stand by your side and in some way help you bear the problems that are the common lot of mankind. "A writer is dear and necessary for us only in the measure in which he reveals to us the inner workings of his soul" (Leo Tolstoi).

Since our lives are the instruments upon which the Great Musician plays, others will sing the songs they hear in our hearts. Someone has said that words are the bridges over which thoughts and feelings pass from one person to another. Within the covers of this book my heart is bared to yours. I still do not completely understand the answer to my mother's **why** nor mine. During so many dark days the encouragement of Christian friends reached out to sustain me and gave me the strength to continue trying. If, in turn, this work can give a ray of hope to someone who has lost heart in wrestling with life's problems and can be influential in helping him struggle to his feet and try again, then perhaps I have found my answer. I could never have reached it without Don, my husband, whose love has made me feel beautiful from within.

Jane McWhorter

1

But God Prepared a Worm... Why?

Poor Jonah had just about **had it**! His anger with God prompted his making a booth for shelter while he waited to see what God would do to Nineveh. In His mercy God lightened the burden of Jonah by causing a gourd to grow as a shadow for this rebellious prophet. **"But God prepared a worm** when the morning rose the next day, and it smote the gourd that it withered" (Jonah 4:7). Why did God deliberately do something which He knew would bring trouble to Jonah?

Why has been a question which has echoed through the ages. The Scriptures are silent concerning the matter, but it is reasonably safe to assume that Adam and Eve must have asked this question when Cain killed Abel. No doubt Noah wondered why his lifetime friends had to die in the flood. Surely Abraham must have questioned God's purpose in demanding the death of Isaac. **Why** did God demand that the blood of the lambs be sprinkled on the doorposts of His people in Egypt? **Why** did He require Naaman to dip **seven** times? While in prison John wondered whether or not this Christ was the promised one (Matthew 11:2,3). Even Christ, with His divine knowledge and understanding, went through mental torture before His own death. At the tomb Peter wondered what was happening (Luke 24:12).

Previous to the beginning of this chapter I included an article which my husband wrote while waiting by my bedside. At the time I was too ill to question **why**; but, as the days lengthened into weeks, the weeks into months, and the months into years, I have had my share of time to meditate and wonder **why**. I wish I could say that I have sailed through without a quiver of the chin or a tear, but I can't. I have wrestled and struggled as I have walked back and forth through the words of Romans 8:28. During past times I suppose I had felt that this verse was a Christian's type of Pollyanna insurance policy which protected him against any harm as long as he was faithful to God. As I searched for a true understanding, I figuratively turned the verse wrong side out. Slowly I began to realize what the Scripture means when it says that all things work together for good to them that love God. The words have been etched into my heart just as emphatically as the Ten Commandments were etched into the tables of stone. It has been a long, slow lesson; but I think I understand much better now. I'd like to share my conclusions with you.

Complete Understanding Impossible

Man's finite mind simply cannot fathom the infinite wisdom of God. God is not on trial in this study any more than Beethoven and his music would be before a band or Shakespeare and his writing before a high school English class.

Deuteronomy 29:29 tells us that the secret things belong to the Lord our God. "For my thoughts are not your thoughts, neither are your ways my ways, saith the Lord. For as the heavens are higher than the earth, so are my ways higher than your ways, and my thoughts than your thoughts" (Isaiah 55:8,9).

Just as a child doesn't reason as an adult, neither do we reason as God does. It has been that way from the beginning. Note these New Testament instances of the difficulties which Christ's followers had in understanding His mission:

1. "Jesus answered and said unto him, what I do thou knowest not now; but thou shalt know hereafter" (John 13:7).
2. The Jews asked Jesus to dispel their doubts: "How long dost thou make us to doubt? If thou be the Christ, tell us plainly" (John 10:24).

3. Christ's followers did not understand how many would be saved (Luke 13:23,24).
4. After all His constant teaching, even the apostles were confused about the nature of the kingdom and the time it would be restored (Acts 1:6,7).
5. "I have yet many things to say unto you, but ye cannot bear them now" (John 16:12).

God did not put us on this earth to be happy. We are here to prepare ourselves for life after death. It doesn't really matter whether we live 50 years or 100. Neither does it matter whether those years are carefree or filled with sorrow. The only consideration of lasting importance is where we spend eternity.

Perhaps our grasp of the situation can best be illustrated by a little story I heard long ago. A parade was progressing down a very long street. God, in His wisdom, could see the entire event from beginning to end. Man had to view the parade through a tiny knothole in the fence. His view was entirely different from that of the One who saw from beginning to end. God can see how events which seem so terrible to us can often make the difference in our eternal destination, which is the only thing of lasting importance. Since we cannot see the entire situation, often we fail to understand. It's difficult to work a puzzle when you don't have all the parts. A mold would seem strange if we had never seen the key made from it. So would a key seem strange if we had never seen a lock. But **our** ignorance does not change the truthfulness of the matter.

Sometimes it seems that those who try the hardest have the most troubles in this life. I have files full of such clippings. Perhaps the question can best be answered by the story of two farmers. One worked in his fields all day on Sundays while the other one took time for a day of worship. The evil man had a better crop when harvesting time came. Why? God doesn't settle all His accounts in October. There **will** be a day of reckoning when the scales will be balanced.

Troubles Promised

Being a child of God has never been assurance that one would be free of difficulties. The wise writer of Ecclesiastes observed in 11:7,8: "Truly the light is sweet, and a pleasant thing it is for the eyes to behold the sun: But if a man live many years, and rejoice in them all; **yet let him remember the days of darkness; for they shall be many.**"

Note the realistic approach that troubles will come to all in these verses:

(1) "Yet man is born unto trouble as the sparks fly upward" (Job 5:7).

(2) "Man that is born of a woman is of few days, and full of trouble" (Job 14:1).

(3) "But his flesh upon him shall have pain, and his soul within him shall mourn" (Job 14:22).

(4) "For all his days are sorrows" (Ecclesiastes 2:23).

(5) "In the world ye shall have tribulation" (John 16:33).

(6) "Yea, and all that will live godly in Christ Jesus shall suffer persecution" (2 Timothy 3:12).

(7) "If any man will come after me, let him deny himself, and take up his cross, and follow me" (Matthew 16:24).

Dilemma

Using human reasoning alone, it would seem that the sufferings of mankind would have to result from one of two reasons. Is God not **powerful** enough to prevent these calamities or is His **love** for us not **sufficient** to spare us from troubles? We'll consider the first part of the dilemma in this chapter and cover the other side in the next chapter. Our finite minds probably could not completely understand even if God Himself sat down to try to explain the reasons. **Why** we have sufferings is not nearly as important as **how** we meet them, but we'll try to get a better grasp of the situation.

Not Powerful Enough?

God is all powerful. "With God all things are possible" (Matthew 19:26). "For with God all things are possible" (Mark 10:27). (Note that both statements were preceded by a discussion of the feasibility of a rich man's salvation.)

God **can** do anything, but He has limited Himself. It is difficult for our human minds to conceive of a God who obeys His own laws and the limitations which He has placed upon Himself. Hebrews 6:18 tells us that it is impossible for God to lie. God cannot be tempted with evil (James 1:31).

To a certain degree, God limited Himself in the garden when man was given the freedom of choice. When Jehovah finished the creation, He felt that it was good (Genesis 1:31). In the midst of the garden were two important trees. Eating of the tree of life would have enabled man to live forever (Genesis 3:22). Partaking of the fruit of the other tree would have given man the ability to discern good and evil (Genesis 2:17). When Eve and Adam chose to eat of the latter, they were cast out of the garden and removed from the possibility of eating of the tree of life and living forever (Genesis 3:22-24). At that moment the dying process began and has continued throughout the ages. Man deserved to be cast off. "For the wages of sin is death" (Romans 6:23). Even though mankind would have to go through the physical ordeal of death (Hebrews 9:27), a plan was devised whereby he could be saved eternally (See Genesis 3:15; Romans 5:8,9; Galatians 4:4-6; Ephesians 1:7; Mark 16:15,16; John 3:16.)

When Adam and Eve sinned, the laws of nature took over, including death-producing diseases and accidents. The laws can be both good and bad, but God limited Himself when He made those laws **consistent**. For example, think how much better the use of **fire** has made man's life; but also consider the destruction it has wrought. When properly controlled, fire is beneficial; but it always burns when it touches flammable objects. Where would we be without the benefits of **steel** in cars and buildings? The same steel can be a means of death when a car is driven improperly or when used in the making of guns. **Wood** can be used to build a shelter for a family or as a club with which to beat someone to death. Victory goes to the strongest, whether the strongest is good or evil. The building of a house would be impossible without the use of a **nail**, but look what this piece of metal did to Sisera (Judges 4:21)! Most people think of **pain** as a nuisance; but, without its warning signals, a person could be cut and bleed to death before he could receive proper attention. **Electricity** cooks our meals, heats our homes, washes and dries our clothes for us in addition to many other benefits; but the power charging through those wires is no respecter of persons. When used without proper precaution, it kills people—both good and evil.

Common sense tells us that these laws of nature must be consistent if they are to be beneficial. What would happen if wood became soft when used as a weapon? What would happen to our communications system if air waves wouldn't function when they carried evil words? We may become irritated when we fall out of a tree, but that same law of gravity prevents our flying off into space. Thus, if we desire to reap the benefits of nature's laws, we must also be prepared to expect some evil consequences.

In addition to realizing that the laws of nature are consistent and no respecter of persons, we must admit that many of mankind's ills can be traced to his own **carelessness** of these laws. Instead of blaming an illness on God, we should be mature enough to admit that failure to properly care for our bodies is often the trouble. Instead of cursing God for letting an automobile accident happen, many times **we** should accept the blame for driving carelessly.

We may be extremely careful and still face difficulties because of yet another natural consequence. We do not live in this world alone. Who would **want** to be deprived of companionship and live completely by himself? "For none of us liveth to himself, and no man dieth to himself" (Romans 14:7). Part of the price of companionship is living with others who are free to "do their own thing." Think how many innocent people are hurt by the acts of others. A drunken driver kills a little child playing near the street. An expectant mother who is hooked on drugs produces a deformed baby. Irresponsible parents may scar their children's minds as well as their bodies. We could go on and on with similar examples. But who would want to live completely alone in order to avoid the consequences of living in a society with others who may intentionally or unintentionally bring harm to their fellow human beings?

In summary, we may say that God **is** all powerful but that He placed certain limitations on Himself when He gave man the freedom to make his own choices. Consequently, the laws of nature must work consistently (for both the good and the evil) if they are to be reliable. Second, our carelessness of these laws causes much of our trouble. Third, living with others necessitates hardships for the innocent.

Freedom is expensive and involves certain dangers. Often parents will give their children allowances in order to teach them efficient money management. There should be freedom to make immature purchases as well as guidance in making wise ones if the child is ever to learn. Learning involves making mistakes. God has given us the freedom to choose, but we must be willing to pay the price—the consequences of natural laws, troubles caused by our own poor reasoning, and suffering due to the thoughtlessness and incompetence of others.

In the next chapter we will consider the other horn of the dilemma: doesn't God **love** us enough to spare us the hardships of suffering?

Suggestions for Class Use
Lesson One

1. Briefly review the story of Jonah with the class. Why do you think God caused the growing of a gourd to shield this prophet from the sun and then prepared a worm to kill the gourd?
2. Name some Bible characters who had good reason to wonder why. (Add to the list in the lesson.)
3. Abraham probably was humanly bewildered over God's command to offer Isaac. From Genesis 22:12 give God's reason.

4. According to Deuteronomy 29:29 and Isaiah 55:8,9 why is it impossible for humans to understand the ways of God?

5. Cite instances to show that even Christ's followers did not understand His mission on earth.

6. Why were we put here? How does this change the significance of troubles?

7. How do you explain Matthew 11:30: "For my yoke is easy, and my burden is light"?

8. From your own experiences, give examples of some good people who have had undeserved misfortunes in this life in addition to some wicked ones who have seemingly had all the good luck. Why does life often turn out in this manner?

9. The word "trouble" has many different connotations. Select one of these definitions and give your own interpretation: trials, tests, temptations, afflictions, infirmities, weaknesses, burdens, anxiety, unrest, pain, mourning, tribulation.

10. What general rule of life does the writer of Ecclesiastes cite in 11:7,8?

11. Give a number of other biblical statements that warn all of us to expect troubles.

12. According to human reasoning, the sufferings of mankind would have to be the result of one of what two reasons?

13. In Matthew 19:26 and Mark 10:27 we learn that with God all things are possible, but in Hebrews 6:18 and James 1:13 God has limited Himself in what two ways? How can God be all powerful and yet have limitations?

14. Discuss the fall of Adam and Eve and the effect which their freedom of choice had on the destiny of all future generations.

15. Add to these examples to prove that the laws of nature must be consistent if they are to be beneficial: fire, steel, wood, pain, electricity.

16. How can our carelessness of nature's laws cause many of our troubles?

17. How can living with others bring harm to innocent people? Would you want to live without human

companionship in order to avoid the risk of suffering the consequences?

18. God **is** all powerful. Summarize the three reasons offered for His failure to spare man from troubles. Add your own suggestions to this list.

19. Do you agree or disagree with the idea that **how** we handle tribulations is more important than **why** we have them?

2
Why? Doesn't God Love Us?

In the previous chapter we learned that man has never completely understood God's methods, but acceptance is far more important than understanding. Troubles are promised. Man cannot expect to live a life of ease. God **is** powerful enough to free man of all troubles, but He limited Himself when He gave mankind freedom of choice and the laws of nature became consistent.

Kindness and Love

Perhaps much of our lack of understanding is the result of a failure to distinguish between the traits of **kindness** and **love**. There is kindness in love but the two are not synonymous. Too many of us seem to have an image of God as a heavenly Santa Claus or a grandfather who passes out toys and candy to good little boys and girls and never disciplines in any way. Such action may be kindness but it is not love. After all, man was not primarily made that he might love God but that God should love him and be well pleased (Revelation 4:11). God's love is completely unselfish. He loved us so much that He gave His only begotten son so we could have eternal life (John 3:16).

Just as a good parent wants his offspring to develop into responsible, unspoiled adults, so does God desire the perfecting of His children. In fact, love **demands** the perfecting of the beloved. Love would rather see a child suffer in order to produce his ultimate good rather than withhold all discipline and watch him grow into a contemptible adult whom no one can tolerate. God wants

what is good for us in the same manner that a parent will
ignore the pleadings of his child for food immediately before
surgery or permit painful injections to cause immunity from
disease.

Benefits of Tribulations

Troubles are promised and we should expect them.
Intellectually we know that these tribulations help make us
better people, but **how** is it done?

(1) **Testing is a part of the Christian life.** When the new
convert comes forth from the watery grave of baptism, he
might as well get his pencil sharpened and his paper ready
because he **will** be tested. Testing is part of the Christian
life and must be expected. Any testing, whether it be oral
or written, is a very valid means of ascertaining how much
the student has learned. When the pupil does a poor job on
a test, a teacher can be fairly certain of one of two things:
his teaching was inadequate or his student did little work in
preparation. The wise writer of Proverbs tells us that if we
faint in the day of adversity, our strength is small
(Proverbs 24:10).

We are told to endure hardness as a good soldier of Jesus
Christ (2 Timothy 2:3). Competition is implied when the
Christian life is referred to as a race (Hebrews 12:1). Job
speaks very plainly of man's being tried (Job 7:18).
Abraham's faith was tried when he was asked to offer Isaac
as a sacrifice. (You could name many more great Bible
characters who went through the agonies of trials.) There is
a difference in a Christian's suffering and that of a sinner. A
Christian suffers for a purpose (1 Peter 4:13,14). Peter also
spoke of the fiery trial of a Christian (1 Peter 4:12). In an
earlier chapter the same writer told the followers of Christ
that they would suffer when they did well (2:20).
Philippians 1:29 states that we will suffer for Christ's sake.

We must remember that our problems are filtered by
God (1 Corinthians 10:13) and no more is put upon us than
we are able to bear. Our ability to properly handle
tribulations increases if our hearts are receptive and our
attitudes are right. The twists and turns of daily living

reveal our inner spirits instead of being the **cause**. Don't fret over burdens. They are indicative of Someone's confidence in your ability. Problems are necessary to one's growth just as exercise is necessary for a baby's proper development. The successful solution to a problem is another rung in the ladder to maturity. In every adversity is the seed of something good. Each hardship should make us better. Someone has said that to realize the worth of the anchor, we must feel the storm. As long as we live purposefully, we will be plunged into the mainstream of life with its inherent tests. Occasionally one will see a completely withdrawn person in a nursing home. The problems of such people are few because they have detached themselves from life. But that really is not living. Neither do we measure a person's ability in life by his attainments as much as by the difficulties he has overcome in reaching that goal.

A Christian never becomes so perfect that he is no longer tested. When he satisfactorily completes one trial and breathes a sigh of relief, another one rears its ugly head and must be dealt with. Often the scar tissue never leaves, but the child of God is made stronger by each successful victory. "God will not look you over for medals, degrees or diplomas, but for scars."

(2) **Suffering causes man to repent, strips him of vanity and pride, and causes him to depend upon God.** Ezra tells us that we are punished less than our iniquities deserve (Ezra 9:13). David realized that he went astray before he was afflicted (Psalms 119:67) and confessed a few verses later that it was good for him to have been afflicted (verse 71). The suffering of the prodigal son no doubt caused him to repent. Romans 2:4 tells us that the goodness of God leads men to repentance. How can both the chastisement of God and His goodness lead to the same end?

God has no place for the proud and the haughty. "Humble yourselves in the sight of the Lord, and he shall lift you up" (James 4:10). "And whosoever shall exhalt himself shall be abased; and he that shall humble himself shall be exalted" (Matthew 23:12). "God resisteth the proud, but giveth grace unto the humble. Submit yourselves therefore to God

. . . Draw nigh to God, and he will draw nigh to you . . . Be afflicted, and mourn, and weep: let your laughter be turned to mourning, and your joy to heaviness. Humble yourselves in the sight of the Lord, and he shall lift you up" (James 4:6-10). Christ's strength was made perfect in weakness (2 Corinthians 12:9). Most of us are not unlike Jonah. Adversity was required before he remembered the Lord (Jonah 2:7). Troubles cause us to lean upon God. "Trust in the Lord with all thine heart; and lean not unto thine own understanding. In all thy ways acknowledge him, and he shall direct thy paths" (Proverbs 3:5,6).

Most humans are too arrogant to be of much use to God. Like the great stones used in making a mighty building, they must be cut and shaped to be of value. We sing loudly that God is the potter and we are the clay. Then we start whimpering when God does a little shaping with our lives. We must willingly give ourselves into the potter's skilled hands before anything of worth can be made of the lump of clay which we call humanity. "God had one Son on earth without sin, but never one without suffering" (Augustine).

So often God wants us to have greater blessings (spiritual ones, such as salvation, character, humility, love, concern for others, appreciation, integrity), but our hands are too full of material possessions and a sense of haughtiness over our own worth (much of which can be attributed to good health, which we take for granted) that there is no room to hold the great blessings which He would like to bestow upon us. Sometimes our hands must be emptied before they can hold things of real importance. Just as Christ's hands were torn by spikes before He was lifted up from the earth, so must our own hands be emptied of worldly possessions and filled with burdens before **we** can be lifted up.

"Wisdom is oftimes nearer when we stoop than when we soar."   William Wordsworth

(3) **Yes, God does chasten us.** Although His natural laws are consistent, there can be no doubt that God works through these laws or by some other means to chasten His children. There are too many Scriptures to deny this fact.

(a) "As a man chasteneth his son, so the Lord thy God chasteneth thee" (Deuteronomy 8:5).

(b) "If he (Solomon) commit iniquity, I will chasten him
with the rod of men, and with the stripes of the
children of men: But my mercy shall not depart
away from him" (2 Samuel 7:14,15).

(c) "My son, despise not the chastening of the Lord;
neither be weary of his correction: for whom the
Lord loveth he correcteth; even as a father the son
in whom he delighteth" (Proverbs 3:11,12).

(d) "The Lord hath chastened me sore" (Psalms
118:18).

(e) "Behold, happy is the man whom God correcteth"
(Job 5:17).

(f) "My son, despise not thou the chastening of the
Lord, nor faint when thou art rebuked of him: For
whom the Lord loveth he chasteneth, and
scourgeth every son whom he receiveth" (Hebrews
12:5,6).

(g) God chastens us for our profit that we might be
partakers of His holiness. "Now no chastening for
the present seemeth to be joyous, but grievous:
nevertheless afterward it yieldeth the peaceable
fruit of righteousness unto them which are
exercised thereby" (Hebrews 12:10,11).

(h) "But when we are judged, we are chastened of the
Lord, that we should not be condemned with the
world" (1 Corinthians 11:32).

(i) 2 Corinthians 6:9 tells us that we are chastened but
not killed.

(j) "As many as I love, I rebuke and chasten"
(Revelation 3:19).

With the abundance of the above cited Scriptures, no one
can deny that God chastens His children much as an earthly
father corrects his children to make them better. Our lack
of understanding of **how** or **why** does not nullify these facts.

(4) **Not all tribulation is the result of man's sin.** "Who-
ever perished, being innocent?" (Job 4:7). Just because the
Scriptures teach that God does chasten His children to
make them better and to strip them of vanity and pride, it
should not be assumed that **all** tribulation is an indication of
a person's sin. Some troubles are the natural result of living

in a world with consistent laws of nature (including disease and its inevitable results) and filled with other people who are free to act as they wish. Christ Himself cited two examples of innocent people who lost their lives in Luke 13:1-5: the Galileans whose blood Pilate mingled with their sacrifices and the 18 upon whom the tower in Siloam fell. The blind man mentioned in John 9:1-3 was not so afflicted because of his own sins. Exodus 20:5 tells us that God visited the iniquity of the fathers upon the third and fourth generations. All could cite examples of children who have suffered as a natural result of the sins of their parents and grandparents. The suffering of many martyrs was brought about, not for wrongdoing, but for the Lord's sake. "But and if ye suffer for righteousness' sake, happy are ye" (1 Peter 3:14).

(5) **Suffering polishes or perfects our Christian characters.** Horace, the great Roman thinker, said that difficulties elicit talents that in more fortunate circumstances would lie dormant. Disraeli, one-time prime minister of Great Britain, believed that difficulties constitute the best education in this life. "Many people owe the grandeur of their lives to their tremendous difficulties" (Charles Spurgeon).

Even though we may be mature in years, most of us have difficulty in understanding how troubles can make us better much as a child has a similar difficulty in comprehending how the spanking which his parent has administered can possibly make him better in years to come. But it does. "For our light affliction, which is but for a moment, worketh for us a far more exceeding and eternal weight of glory" (2 Corinthians 4:17). When we come forth from the watery grave of baptism, we scarcely are finished products. We're more like negatives which have to be developed in a darkroom. Usually that developing process requires years. Diamonds are not polished with velvet but with abrasive elements. Gold is seldom of use in its natural state but must be refined. God's Word repeatedly uses this same comparison.

(a) "Behold, I have refined thee, but not with silver; I have chosen thee in the furnace of affliction" (Isaiah 48:10).

(b) "For thou, O God, has proved us: thou hast tried us, as silver is tried" (Psalms 66:10).

(c) "He shall purify the sons of Levi, and purge them as gold and silver, that they may offer unto the Lord an offering in righteousness" (Malachi 3:3).

(d) Job felt confident that when God had tried him, he would come forth as gold (Job 23:10).

(e) Peter expressed the same thought when he said: "The trial of your faith, being much more precious than of gold that perisheth, though it be tried with fire, might be found unto praise and honor and glory at the appearing of Jesus Christ" (1 Peter 1:7).

We may have trouble understanding, but the Scriptures teach plainly that the trying of our faith works patience (James 1:2,3). "We glory in tribulations also: knowing that tribulation worketh patience" (Romans 5:3). Just as a woman suffers in bringing a child into this world and then forgets the pain when she experiences the joy of her baby, so do Christians forget the pain and anguish when finally they realize the result of their suffering. This joy "no man taketh from you" (John 16:20-22).

Moses was not ready for the tremendous responsibility of leading his people from Egypt when he fled from Pharaoh's court for fear of his life after he had killed the Egyptian. His development required 40 years in the crucible of Midian before he was qualified for the task. This leader had to learn that many battles are not fought with might but with the strength of God.

Perhaps we can better understand how tribulations polish our characters by considering these quotations which have been collected over the years.

1. The caverns of sorrow have mines of diamonds.

2. God sometimes sends His love letters in black-edged envelopes.

3. A pearl is the result of an oyster's irritation.

4. Life is like a grindstone. Whether it polishes us or reduces us to ashes depends upon what we are made of.

5. The Lord sometimes sharpens His saints on the Devil's grindstone.
6. All sunshine makes a desert.
7. If you remove its rocks, the brook will lose its song.
8. When God puts a tear in your eye, it is because He wants to put a rainbow in your heart.
9. God, like a surgeon, could say, "I may hurt you but I will not injure you."
10. Difficulties should make us better, not bitter.
11. No diamond in God's jewel box is ready for display until it is cut, ground and polished.
12. The Lord will mend your broken heart but first you must give Him all the pieces.
13. When the outlook is bad, try the uplook.
14. Courage is fear that has said its prayers.
15. You must be melted before you can be molded.
16. There is nothing more beautiful than a rainbow, but it takes both rain and sunshine to make it.
17. A Christian is much like a kite; only as he is flown against the wind can he rise.
18. What may be bitter to endure is often sweet to remember.
19. Until the colt is broken, it will never pull a load; so, too, God breaks before He makes.
20. Christians are like tea; it takes hot water to bring out their strength.
21. Just as a certain degree of solar heat is necessary to bring the finest fruit to perfection, so are fiery trials indispensable for the ripening of the inner man.
22. God often digs wells of joy with the spade of sorrow.
23. Grief is itself a medicine and food for the soul.
24. Even as the bruised grape gives forth its liquid treasure, so only a broken and contrite heart can yield the fragrant perfume of holiness.
25. As long as you face the light, the dark shadows will always fall behind you.
26. God loves us, not for what we are, but for what He can make of us.
27. Joy frequently needs pain to give it birth.
28. Our Lord is much like a great printer. Often to us the type seems jumbled and backward; however, when we

are "stamped off" over in the other life, all will tell a perfect story.

29. Never put a question mark where God has put a period.
30. Our trouble often is that when trying times come, we stop trying and start crying.
31. Stones in the sea are made smooth by friction.
32. Christians are like violin strings. They will do nothing until they are bound. Then they are free to sing.
33. Roses must be pruned in order to be more beautiful next year.
34. You can't make omelets without breaking eggs.
35. Strength is not born in joy but in the silence of long-suffering hearts.
36. "God brings men into deep waters not to drown them but to cleanse them."

"Difficulty is the nurse of greatness—a harsh nurse, who roughly rocks her foster children into strength and athletic proportion. The mind, grappling with great aims and wrestling with mighty impediments, grows by a certain necessity to their stature" (William Cullen Bryant).

We can go through the experiences of suffering without ever learning the lessons. This is the real tragedy. "With the soul that ever felt the sting of sorrow, sorrow is a sacred thing" (William Cowper).

(6) **Misfortunes better enable us to comfort others.** No one can extend a sympathetic hand as well as one who has experienced the same troubles. We may **think** we know how others feel, but we really don't until we have walked in their shoes and have felt the same rocks in the road. "Blessed be God . . . Who comforteth us in all our tribulation, that we may be able to comfort them which are in any trouble, by the comfort wherewith we ourselves are comforted of God" (2 Corinthians 1:3,4). In Galatians 6:2 we are admonished to bear one another's burdens. We can measure our likeness to Christ by our sensitivity to the trials, pains and loneliness of others.

As more exposed to suffering and distress;
Thence also, more alive to tenderness.
                                William Wordsworth

Love is loveliest when embalmed in tears.
> Sir Walter Scott

Sometimes God puts chains on us in order that we might help others. Just as Paul was chained to the Roman guards and able to get the gospel into Ceasar's court, so are we chained to reach others. Mothers may feel chained to their small children, but look at the wonderful opportunities afforded by such close association. Quite often the wearing of chains, whatever the problems, may actually free us because we realize that we must rise above them.

BEFORE YOU CAN DRY ANOTHER'S TEARS

Let me not live a life that's free
From THE THINGS that draw me close to THEE—
For how can I ever hope to heal
The wounds of others I do not feel—
If my eyes are dry and I never weep,
How do I know when the hurt is deep—
If my heart is cold and it never bleeds,
How can I tell what my brother needs—
For without "crosses to carry" and "burdens to bear,"
We dance through a life that is frothy and fair,
And "chasing the rainbow" we have no desire
For "roads that are rough" and "realms that are higher"—So spare me no heartache or sorrow, dear Lord,
For the heart that is hurt reaps the richest reward,
And God enters the heart that is broken with sorrow
As He opens the door to a BRIGHTER TOMORROW,
For only through tears can we recognize
The suffering that lies in another's eyes.
> Helen Steiner Rice

(7) **Suffering causes us to yearn for something better as we gain a new perspective.** "For our light affliction, which is but for a moment, worketh for us a far more exceeding and eternal weight of glory" (2 Corinthians 4:17). Paul admonished the Romans in 8:18, "For I reckon that the sufferings of this present time are not worthy to be compared with the glory which shall be revealed in us."

Common sense tells us that nothing but joy and pleasure in this life would only intensify our desire to remain here forever. When we suffer, we are lifted above the world as we learn that there is something more important and wonderful than our brief sojourn on this earth. As we long for a better life, we are gradually detached from the things of this world.

Like Abraham, we look for a city with foundation (Hebrews 11:10). With Paul we can say that we are miserable if we have hope only in this life (1 Corinthians 15:19). Christians look for a house not made with hands (2 Corinthians 5:1-4). Every tribulation that a child of God faces makes the words of Revelation 21:4 become a little sweeter and more meaningful each time they are read: "And God shall wipe away all tears from their eyes; and there shall be no more death, neither sorrow, nor crying, neither shall there be any more pain: for the former things are passed away."

When we are in the midst of all the **things** of this earth, many trivialities seem so important. For example, when one lies on the ground on a summer day, a tiny beetle may appear very large as it rests on a blade of grass. As we leave the grassy fields and climb to a mountain nearby, the beetle cannot even be seen and loses its importance in relationship to the entire landscape. To an average family, the buying of a new car or a new house may seem very important; but the serious illness of a child in that family very quickly helps each member to view life in its proper perspective. Then the new car or the new house does not seem nearly as important as before.

When I first left the hospital, I'll never forget the words of my plastic surgeon. He told me that it had been a long, hard struggle but that the road now was all downhill. I am now down among the beetles and other daily cares, but I am thankful that for one period of time in my life I had the opportunity to climb the mountain and get things in their proper perspective. When I become bogged down with all of life's trivia, I have to occasionally take a mental trip to the top of that mountain to get my sense of values in order.

> The Lord God is my strength, and he
> will make my feet like hinds' feet,
> and he will make me to walk upon mine
> high places.
>
> Habakkuk 3:19

Suggestions for Class Use
Lesson Two

1. Briefly summarize the important points made in the previous chapter. Divide into seven groups to discuss each of the reasons listed in Lesson Two or use the following questions in a general class discussion.
2. What is the difference in kindness and love? What part do the two have in the rearing of children?
3. Why is testing a part of the Christian life? Why should anyone feel that God has turned against him when his faith is put to the test?
4. What is the difference in the suffering of a Christian and that of a sinner?
5. According to 1 Corinthians 10:13, what happens to problems before they are sent our way?
6. Do you agree or disagree? Burdens are indicative of God's confidence in your ability.
7. Compare our problems with the exercise needed for a baby's growth.
8. Which is more important: to measure a person's ability in life by his attainments or by the difficulties which he has overcome in reaching his goal?
9. How can suffering cause us to repent and be made humble?
10. Cite examples of Bible characters who repented because of troubles.
11. How can both the chastisement of God and His goodness lead to the same end?
12. Discuss Proverbs 3:5,6 to prove that troubles cause us trust in God instead of our own understanding.

13. Shadrach, Meshach and Abednego said that their God was able to deliver them (Daniel 3:17). How were they delivered? Did they have to go through the ordeal?

14. Why do we require some shaping and chiseling before we can be of real value to the Lord in His service?

15. Prove by the Scriptures that God does chasten us.

16. Does suffering automatically indicate that the afflicted one has merited the punishment by some wrong-doing? What are some other reasons? Cite Biblical examples of the suffering of innocent people.

17. In a number of instances God's Word compares suffering with the refining of what precious metal?

18. James 1:2,3 states that the trying of our faith worketh patience. How can this be possible?

19. Assign the quotations in section five to various class members for comment.

20. Use 2 Corinthians 1:3,4 and Galatians 6:2 to prove that tribulations enable us to be more sympathetic toward our fellow-man. Illustrate with personal examples.

21. If we had no troubles on this earth, would we ever want to leave? What is awaiting those who patiently endure and obey? (See 2 Corinthians 4:17 and Romans 8:18.)

22. How can burdens help us gain a better perspective of life and understand what is truly important? How can "getting away from it all" help us straighten out our sense of values?

3

How Can We Prepare Before Troubles Come?

Troubles have plagued mankind since the dawn of history. Each age has its own specific problems which act as stimuli to growth. Humans need hurdles to jump in order to grow. The higher the hurdle, the bigger the jump. To deny the presence of tribulations would be much like an ostrich hiding its head in the sand. If sorrows and troubles have not knocked at your door yet, they are just down the street. Christians are to put on the proper armor to enable them to fight the battle of life successfully (Ephesians 6:11).

Someone has said that there's nothing in life we need to fear; it's just to be **understood** because fear springs from ignorance. The two previous chapters have presented the reasons behind troubles. Even though we may not **completely** understand, perhaps we are a little closer to the goal. At least we can accept in faith. Now the problem is **how** to prepare for adversity and be victorious in the battle.

God saves us from defeat, not from troubles. WE never escape problems; we simply learn how to solve them. No person is completely happy all the time. Trouble and happiness are both at our doorstep. It is left up to us to decide which one will enter and be prominent. Burdens will either **shatter** or **strengthen** our faith, depending upon what is inside.

Perhaps this lesson will give someone the key to the door which he has previously been trying to knock down.

Prepare Before The Battle

Once a general was asked how his battles were won; he replied that they were won the **day before**. How true! We are very careful to nourish our children because we realize that they will one day be adults, and the manner in which the child is treated will be a determining factor in the development of the future adult. By the same comparison, the nature of the future will be greatly influenced by the manner in which we treat the present.

"I thought we shouldn't worry about the future," someone is quick to retort. There is a vast difference between **worry** and **preparation.** "Worry is a thin stream of fear, which, if allowed to trickle through the mind, soon cuts a channel into which all thoughts flow." The word **worry** is combined from two words that mean **mind** and **divide;** it literally means to divide the mind. The original Anglo-Saxon word meant choke or strangle. Worry is the mental attitude of continually **dwelling** upon something undesirable which could possibly come to pass. We practice worry until we become quite adept and it becomes an automatic reflex, which must be consciously broken by substituting constructive thoughts. Whatever we feed and exercise will grow, whether it be faith or doubt. Worry is like a dog chasing his own tail. He gets nowhere but uses all his energy. Just as a bow will break if it is always stretched, so will a person break if he is constantly in a state of worry.

Instead of worrying about the future, **plan** for it. No one should learn to sail a boat in a storm; neither should anyone try to learn how to solve problems while in the midst of them. A great violinist doesn't step out on the concert stage before an audience without many years of preparation. Far too many Christians not only have made little preparation to meet life's trials, but they also try to play the melody of life on untuned instruments. Then they wring their hands and wonder why fate has dealt them such unfavorable blows. I've always had very little patience with pupils in school who do not even have enough concern to study for the questions which I had previously told them would be on the test. God has told us we will be tested. It is **our** responsibility to make proper preparation.

How do we prepare? Most of the time we underestimate ourselves and overestimate the difficulty. Instead of constantly worrying about the future, stop and ask yourself this question: what is the **worst** thing that could happen concerning this particular problem? Then, calmly and rationally, consider all possible alternatives and decide what would be your **best** course of action. After thinking about it for several days to be reasonably certain you've made the right decision, **forget** about it! You've already planned the most intelligent course you could follow. What else **is** there to do? At least 90 percent of the bad things which we think might happen to us never come to pass; hence the odds are in our favor.

I well remember a ladies' class taught by Mrs. Elvis Huffard. She told of her reaction when her husband informed her that they were being sent to Sierra Leone, Africa for a year. When they got on the plane, she thought: "What will I do if this thing goes down over the ocean?" She decided that the only thing she **could** do would be to cry and scream and get her family on one of the life-boats. Then she said she forgot about it. Next she thought: "What will I do if the only place we can find to live looks terrible?" She tried to think of the worst building she could imagine. The picture of an abandoned service station came to her mind. She reasoned that she would get some whitewash, make curtains, and put flowers in the windows. Then she forgot about those problems. Emily had made the best decisions when she was not under pressure and could think rationally. Fortunately, she did not have to resort to either course of action.

Perhaps we can better understand the benefits of thinking ahead if we know how the mind works. When we are not under pressure, we can usually depend upon the conscious part of the brain to do the reasoning. When we are under stress, however, we tend to react with the subconscious and rely upon habits used to meet similar situations earlier in life. A habit is an automatic response. A good example would be the mechanics of driving a car. The best course of action is to groove desirable traits into our brains by constant practice so we will take the right action without even thinking about it. I have read that the astronauts are so well trained for emergencies that their blood pressure doesn't even rise when they blast off. The principle of practice without pressure can be seen in many everyday examples. This is the rationale behind fire drills

at school. A golf expert will swing at an imaginary ball
many times. Shadow boxing is used by fighters. During
such practices, a mental map is formed in the brain in order
that a person may react correctly without conscious effort.

There's nothing we can do about our heredity.
Frequently there's little we can do to change our
environment. But we do have the control of our personal
response to the first two factors. We are not marionettes.

Trust in God Through His Word

Like giant oak trees, we should lift our branches to the
sky and send our roots to the ground to secure the strength
we will need when the storms of life come. That strength is
not self-generated any more than is one able to pull himself
out of quicksand; it is assimilated from a higher source.
Since the perfect law of liberty has come (James 1:25), we
connect to our source of power through His Word. The
Scriptures abound with promises that God is with His
children in their troubles.

"The Lord thy God is with thee whitersoever thou goest"
   (Joshua 1:9).
"God is our refuge and strength, a very present help in
   trouble" (Psalms 46:1).
"I will never leave thee, nor forsake thee"
   (Hebrews 13:5).
"Humble yourselves therefore under the mighty hand of
   God, that he may exalt you in due time: Casting all
   your care upon him; for he careth for you"
   (1 Peter 5:6,7).
"Underneath are the everlasting arms" (Deuteronomy
   33:27).
"Cast thy burden upon the Lord, and he shall sustain
   thee" (Psalms 55:22).
"If God be for us, who can be against us?" (Romans 8:31).
"For I the Lord thy God will hold thy right hand, saying
   unto thee, Fear not; I will help thee" (Isaiah 41:13).

Space will not permit direct quotations, but the following passages are filled with similar thoughts: Romans 4:21; Luke 12:22-31; Proverbs 3:6; Psalms 31:15; Romans 8:28-39;Deuteronomy 4:30,31; Psalms 121:1,2; Psalms 31:7; Job 35:10; 1 Samuel 30:6; Psalms 119:92.

Too many of us **intellectually** believe the above passages but don't **emotionally** accept them. We're too much like the man with the heavy load who was given a ride in a wagon. When the farmer asked the man why he didn't put his sack down on the wagon bed, he replied that he didn't think the farmer wanted to carry both the man and his sack; so he was still holding on to the load!

Strength from God's Word is available, but we have to plant it in our minds before trouble comes; seeds require time to germinate. If we want to have a spiritual bank account from which to withdraw, we must make regular deposits. God adds the interest.

The Israelites had very strict commands concerning the teaching of the Scriptures (Proverbs 6:20-23). The Word has to be hidden in our hearts (Psalms 119:11) in order that it will be deeply implanted as a part of our subconscious minds in time of need. Christ learned the Scriptures at a very early age and was found quoting some of these verses during His temptation (Deuteronomy 8:3; Deuteronomy 6:13; Psalms 91:11,12) and on the cross (Psalms 22:1; Psalms 31:5).

Troubles will still come; but, like Shadrach, Meshach, and Abednego, someone will walk with us through any fiery furnace we have to face (Daniel 3:25). **We** will still have to endure hardships, but the difference between the plight of a Christian and an unbeliever is that a child of God will never have to face anything alone. This illustration may be crude, but I think it helps to get the point across. Several months ago, I had cut my finger and wore a bandage for several days. When I was doing some writing with a pen, I removed the bandage but found that the finger was still too sore to hold the pen. I could write just fine when I put on another bandage. What was the difference? The pen was still there, just the same. My finger still had its soreness. But now I had something to shield me. In like manner, although we will have burdens to bear all our lives, we will not feel as much pain and agony because we have Someone to go between us and the source of irriation for protection. "But thou, O Lord, art a shield for me" (Psalms 3:3).

I know not where His islands lift
Their fronded palms in air;
I only know I cannot drift
Beyond His love and care.
                    John Greenleaf Whittier

Learn How To Pray

God speaks to us through His Word; we talk to Him through prayer. Years ago Alfred, Lord Tennyson observed: "More things are wrought by prayer than this world dreams of."

"What things soever ye desire, when ye pray, believe that ye receive them, and ye shall have them" (Mark 11:24). "Ye ask, and receive not, because ye ask amiss, that ye may consume it upon your lusts" (James 4:3). Far too many Christians have the wrong concept of prayer. They view it in a magical sense, as if they could say OPEN SESAME and their wishes would be automatically granted. Christ begged: "Let this cup pass," but He also understood the conditions: "Nevertheless not as I will, but as **thou** wilt" (Matthew 26:39). We must understand that God is more interested in making us what we **ought** to **be** than He is in giving us what we would **like** to **have.** Joseph realized that God meant all of His servant's hardships for good (Genesis 50:20). How tragic it would be if we received everything we asked for. I don't believe I am too different from most of you readers. I have, on a number of occasions, asked God for things which were refused. I was crushed at the time but later found that my requests would have been curses instead of blessings. My prayers have most certainly been answered; but sometimes the answer has been, "No, it is not best, My child" or "It is not yet time. Be patient." Instead of going to God in prayer with orders for our wishes, we should pray that we will be channels for whatever is best.

Earlier in our lesson we observed that one shouldn't learn how to sail a boat in a storm. Neither should one try to pray only when he is in trouble. Search the Gospels for the numerous instances for Christ's prayers. When the time came for Him to shoulder His heaviest burden, He resorted to His regular custom (Luke 22:39). Learn to pray properly early in your Christian life so the lines of communication will be open and clear in times of stress. Do you believe in prayer - **really** believe in it?

"Keep your knees down, and your chin up."
"We must get down on our knees
if we hope to get back on our feet."
"It is the uplifted face that feels the shining of the sun."

Develop An Inner Calm

A time of crisis is **not** the time to "get hold of yourself." Isaiah said that in quietness and in confidence would be our strength (Isaiah 30:15). All of us would like to remain calm and unchanging during a storm, but that calmness and strength have to be found ahead of time. Just as a turbulent sea leaves the deepest part of the ocean undisturbed, so should troubles fail to shatter the inner core of a Christian. The writer of Proverbs stated that "he that ruleth his spirit (is better) than he that taketh a city" (Proverbs 16:32). It was Matthew Arnold who said: "He who finds himself, loses his misery." Most of us don't need to "get away from it all." We just need to find a haven within our hearts. Synthesizing our impulses, purposes, emotions, desires and thoughts into a unified personality is no easy task; but a unified attack will help us win our battles much more quickly than when we go to pieces. After all, it is really up to us. We can focus the different parts of our personalities as a bayonet or spread them like a broom. Frankly, I'd rather go into a battle with a bayonet.

Thomas Huxley said, "A man's worst difficulties begin when he is able to do as he likes." As a person's freedom increases, so do his internal conflicts. A Christian is free, but only in the right channel. He has a goal in life. He knows the direction in which he is headed. Perseverance toward that goal keeps him on the right path when the winds of trouble try to blow him away. His determination to reach Heaven is so strong that he refuses to allow anything to get him off his course. Robert Louis Stevenson said, "The habit of being happy enables one to be freed, or largely freed, from the domination of outward conditions." Although his viewpoint is correct, don't forget that the only way to be truly happy is to lose oneself in a cause that is eternal and will go on living long after death. It is **true** Christianity that causes a person to maintain an inner calm no matter what is on the outside, just as the body maintains an even temperature in spite of the weather. Christ can help us exchange spines made of boiled macaroni for backbones strong enough to enable us to hold our heads up, regardless of what happens.

In an attempt to entertain his son, a father tore a page from a magazine with a map of the world printed on it. After ripping the paper into little bits, he offered his son 25 cents to put it back together. The father was very surprised when his boy completed the task in only a few minutes. When asked how we did it, the son replied that there was a picture of a man on the other side. He put the man together, turned it over, and there was the completed map. His explanation was, "I figured that if I got the man right, the world would be right." Out of the mouths of babes. . .

Develop Christian friendships

Even though today's world is filled with people rubbing shoulders with one another, many are very lonely. Being in the presence of others does not insure companionship. Very fortunate indeed is the person who feels that he has several friends - **real** friends with whom he can express his true feelings. "A friend is one who walks in when the rest of the world walks out." How wise the writer of Ecclesiastes was when he wrote: "Two are better than one . . . For if they fall, the one will lift up his fellow: but woe to him that is alone when he falleth; for he hath not another to help him up" (4:9,10). "To him that is afflicted pity should be shewed from his friend" (Job 6:14).

Every Christian can turn to God in prayer during times or troubles and He is certainly the most beloved friend a person will ever have. But we are humans, and we need another human with whom to exchange understanding glances and hear his voice. No one can give us the moral support and words of guidance which we need except another Christian, for others do not have the same set of standards. Unbelieving friends are just about as comforting as Eliphaz, Bildad and Zophar were to Job. The proper time to cultivate Christian friendship is **before** trouble strikes so we can feel comfortable around such people and free to express our feelings.

Christ Himself knew the value of Christian companionship. Twelve men were selected as His companions for three years. During this time He was teaching and training them to carry on His work, but they also fulfilled one of His needs - human friendship. Just as we feel closer to some of our friends than to others, so did Christ feel closer to three - Peter, James and John. The Master knew that the apostles themselves could do better work if they had companionship; consequently, they were sent out two by two (Mark 6:7). Friends do not simply fall into our laps. Friendships must be cultivated. Emerson said: "Man surrounds himself with the true image of himself. We reflect the image which we have of ourselves. If we respect ourselves and others, love them, and accept them, they will react to us in a friendly manner." Centuries before Emerson lived, the writer of Proverbs said: "A man that hath friends must shew himself friendly" (Proverbs 18:24).

One of the primary values of Christian friendship is the manner in which such companions act as conductors of our feelings. Troubles will come to all of us. As long as they flow **through** us, little harm will be done. Difficulties arise, however, when these burdens meet with resistance and stay bottled up inside. Friends are to our emotional houses what good conductors are to the house in which we live. Often they are directly responsible for keeping the house from burning down. We should let our worries flow out in proportion to the amount flowing in.

In my files I have a most touching clipping from a newspaper. It is a picture of two men running a seven-mile

race in which they finished somewhere in the middle of four
thousand participants. They ran the entire race arm in arm.
One was blind. The other was born without hands or feet.
Alone, neither of them would have had a chance. Together
they could conquer a seemingly impossible task.

In the beginning of the third chapter of Ecclesiastes the
writer tells us that there is a time and place for so many
things. Christian companionship is necessary, both in good
and bad times; but the mature child of God realizes that
there are some things which he must face alone. (In the
garden there was a point beyond which not even Christ's
closest three friends could accompany Him.) Sometimes we
are victims of loneliness when we truly need companionship. There are other times, however, when we all need the
healing qualities of solitude. Somehow we must learn to
achieve a mature balance between the two.

In summary we may say that we can prepare for troubles
before they come by planning the best line of defense
against the worst thing that could happen to us and then
forget about it. Second, learn to trust in God through His
Word. Third, develop an active prayer life. Fourth, develop
an inner calm, a stability in life. Fifth, develop strong
Christian friendships. All these characteristics will be
needed **when** adversities strike, but the foundation must
already be there.

Suggestions for Class use
Lesson Three

1. Cite examples from secular history to illustrate the
   point that problems have prodded mankind to great
   discoveries.
2. On the board sketch a soldier in his armor. Discuss the
   various pieces and the comparison to a Christian's
   armor which Paul made in Ephesians 6:10-17. Why
   does a child of God need armor?
3. Do you agree or disagree with the statement: we never
   escape problems; we simply learn how to solve them?
   Compare this with Paul's attitude in 2 Corinthians
   4:8-10.

4. How would you use Job's statement in Job 2:10: "Shall we receive good at the hand of God, and shall we not receive evil?" to strengthen someone who felt that he had been treated unjustly by God?
5. What are the advantages of preparing for adversities before they strike?
6. Use Ecclesiastes 10:8-11 to support Galatians 6:7.
7. Have each class member write a definition of worry on a slip of paper. Collect these and discuss. Include the definitions of worry mentioned in the lesson.
8. What is the difference between worry and preparation?
9. What is the **logical** way to prepare for trouble? (This would be a good question for the class members to discuss in pairs before a general group discussion.)
10. In times of stress the mind generally does not reason; it reacts. How can we program our minds to respond in the best manner? How did Uzzah react? (See 2 Samuel 6:6,7.)

   (Note: frequently class members who are hesitant to speak out in a large group will express their viewpoints readily in a smaller, informal atmosphere. You may deem it best to divide them into four smaller groups to discuss the four suggested methods of preparing for troubles before they arise. The following questions may be used either in the smaller groups as a basis for discussion or in a large class.)

Trust In God Through His Word

11. Why is it so foolish to wait until trouble comes before searching God's Word for an answer?
12. Why does our comfort have to come from a source higher than ourselves?
13. Assign the various class members these passages to read and discuss: Joshua 1:9; Psalms 46:1; Hebrews 13:5; 1 Peter 5:6,7; Deuteronomy 33:27; Psalms 55:22; Romans 8:31; Isaiah 41:13; Romans 4:21; Luke 12:22-31; Proverbs 3:6; Psalms 31:15; Romans 8:28-39; Deuteronomy 4:30,31; Psalms 121:1,2; Psalms 31:7; Job 35:10; 1 Samuel 30:6; Psalms 119:92.

14. How would you explain Psalms 37:5 to one who is blaming his troubles on God?

15. The Word of God is referred to as seeds (Matthew 13:3-9). Seeds require time to germinate. Make the comparison with the words in the Scriptures.

16. Discuss the manner in which Christ used Scriptures in His life.

17. Since Christians still have to endure hardships, of what benefit is God's help through His Word?

Learn How To Pray

18. God speaks to us through His Word. How do we talk to Him?

19. Mark 11:24 says: "What things soever ye desire, when ye pray, believe that ye receive them, and ye shall have them." When a Christian is confused and in doubt because he believes that God failed to answer his prayer, how would you use these passages to help him develop a more mature understanding: James 4:3; 1 Peter 3:12; 2 Chronicles 33:9-13; Hebrews 4:16; 1 John 5:14; Philippians 4:6; Psalms 34:15, 17; James 5:16; Psalms 145:18; Psalms 37:4,5?

20. Christ prayed fervently, but He understood the conditions. What were they?(See Matthew 26:39.)

21. Before the class, assign a special report to be made on the prayer life of Christ.

22. Give as examples some of your prayers which would have been harmful if they had been answered as you requested.

23. Ask yourself how much time you usually spend in prayer. What do you plan to do to improve your prayer life? ("Pray when you feel like it and when you don't.")

Develop An Inner Calm

24. When is the best time to develop an inner calm?

25. Compare a Christian with the deepest part of the ocean.

26. Why is a person who rules his spirit better than he that taketh a city? (See Proverbs 16:32.)

27. Is your inner personality more comparable to a bayonet or a broom?

28. Do you agree or disagree with this statement: as a person's freedom increases, so do his internal conflicts? Compare this with John 8:32.
29. Discuss the illustration of the boy with the puzzle.

Develop Christian Friendships
30. Ecclesiastes 4:9,10 states that two are better than one. What is the reason given?
31. Every Christian has God as his dearest friend. Why does he also need human companionships? Why did Christ need friends? Who were His closest ones?
32. Troubles will come to us all. Why is it best to let them flow **through** us?
33. What place does solitude play in our lives? How can the mature Christian achieve a balance between solitude and companionship? Galatians 6:5 tells every man to bear his own burdens. Galatians 6:2 admonishes Christians to bear one another's burdens. Psalms 55:22 urges the children of God to cast their burdens upon the Lord. How do you reconcile these three thoughts?

4

How Can We Handle Problems When They Come?

By the rivers of Babylon, there we
sat down, yea, we wept, when we
remembered Zion. We hanged our harps
upon the willows in the midst thereof.
For there they that carried us away
captive required of us a song . . . **How
shall we sing the Lord's song in a
strange land?**

Psalms 137:1-4

It is necessary to make preparations before troubles
come, and some suggestions were given in the previous
chapter. When problems hit us in the face, what do we do
then?

Learn to Express Emotions Properly

Our feelings must have expression, or they
will be as clouds, which till they descend
in rain, will never bring up fruit or flower.

H. W. Beecher

A Christian need not feel that he is going to meet every
hurdle without fear or doubts. Such is impossible because
each of us is only human. Christ was the Son of God living in
a human body. If **He** went through such agony in the garden
that an angel from Heaven was sent to strengthen Him
(Luke 22:43), why should **we** be ashamed when we have
trouble accepting hardships? There is nothing wrong with

saying, "Father, I am bewildered and confused. Please help me understand and bear this tribulation." If we accept such an attitude, our faith will become stronger than ever because it has doubted and tested.

Mark Twain wisely observed: "Courage is resistance to fear, mastery of fear—not absence of fear." An unknown sage once remarked: "Courage is fear that has said its prayers."

So many suffer from a vague uneasiness without ever realizing the true cause simply because they are afraid to openly admit their problems to themselves. Instead of repressing our fears until they gnaw at our insides, it is far better to say what they are with our lips. Such can be a wonderful catharsis for our emotions. Steam from a teakettle can either make it sing or explode. Although a skilled plastic surgeon did a wonderful job in reconstructing a new face for me, I was still emotionally hurt over the changes; but I felt a sense of guilt over such thoughts since I had been given the gift of life. After approximately two years, however, I was able to actually say with my lips, "Isn't what happened to my face enough? Why do I have to hurt all the time, too?" Acceptance began its healing process at that moment. An unchangeable situation must be accepted before rebuilding can begin. There is a difference between acceptance and apathy. The latter doesn't distinguish between what can and what cannot be changed. Acceptance does. It is just as important to learn what we cannot do as it is to know what we can do.

Carry Only One Day's Burdens At A Time

Most of us struggle down the road of life with three heavy sacks upon our backs: yesterday's cares wrapped in heavy blankets of guilt for failing to have done better; today's burdens; and tomorrow's imagined troubles, magnified tenfold. No wonder we stay tired all the time!

Christians have a way to drop the sack of yesterday. God has provided forgiveness when we properly confess our faults (James 5:16). When we make restitution to those we have wronged, we should **forget** the matter. It was William

James who said, "The Lord may forgive our sins, but the nervous system never does." The same principle applies to seeming injustices which **we** have received in the past. Forget them! Too many save emotional trading stamps just as they do stamps from the grocery store until they have collected enough books to trade in for a nervous breakdown.

Others take great delight in worrying about the future - all the bad things that **might** happen. In reality, most of those things never come to pass. The French philosopher, Montaigne, aptly observed: "My life has been full of terrible misfortunes most of which never happened."

You have probably heard of the grandfather clock which stopped one day because it realized that during the next 90 years it would tick 2,838,240,000 times. When someone reminded the clock that it would only have to tick once at a time, it had the courage to start again. Today we only have to bear the present burdens, not those of yesterday nor tomorrow. Matthew 6:34 states: "Sufficient unto the day is the evil thereof." We could also say: "Sufficient unto the day is the strength thereof." Living today to the best of our ability helps to make our tomorrows easier to bear. Thomas Carlyle said: "Our main business is not to see what lies dimly at a distance but to do what lies clearly at hand." Sir William Osler , who organized the John Hopkins School of Medicine, advised his Yale students to learn to live one day at a time by making this comparison. He told them to imagine that they were on an ocean liner. First, see that everything is in good working order. Then touch a button and hear the iron doors shutting off the Past. Touch another button and seal off the Future. Learn to live in "day-tight" compartments.

We live our lives just as the grains of sand pass through an hourglass in single file. God gives life to us in stages - one day at a time. Each of us can live only **one** day victoriously. Just as the sand piles up at the bottom of the hourglass, so do our victorious days pile up - one upon another - to make a victorious life. Thirty years before the birth of Christ the Roman poet Horace said: "Tomorrow, do thy worst, for I have liv'd today."

Part of the poem "Salutation to the Dawn" by the Indian
dramatist Kalidasa contains these words:

For yesterday is but a dream
And tomorrow is only a vision,
But today well lived makes every
yesterday a dream of happiness
And every tomorrow a vision of hope.

Remember, no matter how bitter yesterday may have
been nor how burdensome today might be, there is always
the **hope** of tomorrow.

"Finish each day and be done with it. You have done what
you could. Some blunders and absurdities no doubt crept in;
but forget them as soon as you can. Tomorrow is a new day;
begin it well and serenely, and with too high a spirit to be
cumbered with your old nonsense" (Emerson).

Transcend troubles

When some sort of hardship actually hits, there are three
ways in which it may be met. (Actually, there are four; but
we won't even consider ignoring the problem because that's
no solution.)

(1) The most logical course of action is to meet troubles
head-on. Like Caleb, we must often say, "Give me this
mountain" (Joshua 14:12). Admit what the adversity is and
pull from your subconscious your preplanned course of
action. For example, if your physician informs you that
surgery is needed, pretending that the problem isn't there
will only make matters worse. Do whatever has to be done
as soon as possible. I have been told that during
winter storms most cattle will turn their backs and drift
downward until they reach the fence where they pile up and
die. Hereford cattle, on the other hand, head into the storm,
stand shoulder to shoulder with their heads down against it,
and most of them live. I'm certain that many remember
Aesop's fable about the two frogs who fell into a pot of milk.
The pessimist gave up and drowned. The optimist,
however, refused to give up and decided to just swim
around until his strength failed because that was all he
could do. The more he swam, the more the cream turned
into butter. When he had churned enough butter, this
ingenious creature merely hopped out of the bowl from the

top of the butter which he had churned! We can learn some valuable lessons from cattle and frogs.

(2) Let's face reality. There are **some** problems about which we can do nothing, at least not at the present time. To try to face them head-on would be futile. Again, nature gives a good illustration. When a heavy snowstorm hits a forest, many of the stately hardwood trees break under the load of snow and ice and crash to the ground. The pine, however, gracefully bows its branches under the strain. When warmer weather comes and the snow melts, this tree is able to resume its former position because it was flexible.

Some things in this life are worth fighting for. Others are really not that important. We should have the maturity to realize the difference and give a little when necessary. This attribute requires belief that in the end things will work out for the best (Romans 8:28). We pray for a solution to a problem and want it immediately; but often God says WAIT. Patience is doing something constructive in the meantime. "Rest in the Lord, and wait patiently for him" (Psalms 37:7). "But if we hope for that we see not, then do we with patience wait for it" (Romans 8:25). "And let us not be weary in well doing: for in due season we shall reap, if we faint not" (Galatians 6:9). "When ye do well, and suffer for it, ye take it patiently, this is acceptable with God" (1 Peter 2:20). "They that wait upon the Lord shall renew their strength" (Isaiah 40:31). The unpleasant things in this life are so noisy that we frequently forget the silent operation of what is best. Remember that with time and patience the mulberry leaf becomes silk. "Patience is the ability to let your light shine after your fuse has blown."

(3) There are other problems which cannot be met head-on. Patience in waiting for something better to happen is useless because the situation will never change. If the circumstances cannot be changed, then we'll just have to change our attitudes and rise above tribulations just as an airplane rises above the storm clouds into the sunshine. We can voice the sentiments of Frances of Assisi, who said years ago: "God grant me the serenity to accept the things I cannot change, the courage to change the things I can, and the wisdom to know the difference."

The real people to be admired are those who have been
trapped in circumstances over which they had no control
and yet transcend the difficulties to become the victors. It
was Booker T. Washington who spoke of "the advantage of
disadvantages."

If the facts cannot be changed, then we must change our
attitudes toward these facts. For example, some of us may
be totally unable to alter the **fact** that we have suffered
great financial loss. The manner in which we face that fact
is our attitude. There is no need to add our pity and
resentment to bad circumstances. We may not be able to
change the fact, but we will be much happier if we do not
feel that we have been **ruined** by the situation. We **do** have
control over over attitudes, our manner of acceptance.
Montaigne, the French philosopher, supported this theory
with his statement: "A man is not hurt so much by what
happens, as by his opinion of what happens." The blind
writer John Milton said, "It is not miserable to be blind, it is
only miserable to endure blindness." Some people thrive on
molehills and seem to enjoy magnifying every trouble that
comes along.

Affliction may color our lives, but we can choose the
colors. Do roses have thorns or do thorns have roses?
Which is your viewpoint? Happiness is internal and based
upon ideas, thoughts, and attitudes - not things. Abraham
Lincoln summed it up very well when he said: "Most people
are about as happy as they make up their minds to be." No
one can be happy all the time (George Bernard Shaw said
we would probably be miserable if we were), but most of us
can learn to cultivate pleasant thoughts most of the time.

Fortunately, we are not the keys on the piano but the
players. The melody of our lives will be determined by the
manner in which we play those keys. Neither are we
thermometers that register degrees of heat or cold; we are
the thermostats that **control** the temperature. Unlike any
other living creature, man has the ability to elevate his life
by conscious effort. "When you need a helping hand, look at
the end of your arm."

The word **crisis** comes from a Greek word meaning
decisiveness, point of decision. When our direct action will

do nothing to solve a problem, when yielding to the circumstances in patient waiting will not alter the situation, then we have reached a crisis, a point of decision.We can either be overwhelmed and resign ourselves to fate, wallowing in self-pity and resentment for the rest of our lives, or we can accept the **challenge of restrictions.** It was Dr. Alfred Adler who spoke of the human being's power to turn a minus into a plus. Julius Rosenwald, once president of Sears, Roebuck and Company, stated the same idea in clearer terms when he suggested: "When you have a lemon, make lemonade."

It is restrictions that make any work of art meaningful. A violinist must produce beautiful melodies by using four strings. A poet must express his thoughts through the rhythm of words. A sculptor is constrained by the hardness of stone. It is said that Michelangelo saw in every rough block of stone a thing of beauty awaiting the master-hand to bring it into reality. The artist must learn to express himself by means of canvas and pigments. Recently I noticed a newspaper article concerning an artist who uses a magnifying glass and a human eyelash to paint landscapes and portraits on the heads of pins! An actor is restricted by the role which he plays. The circumstances of life may have cast us into parts that do not seem very glamorous, but that is not important. Some are rich; others are poor. Some are healthy; others are sick. Some are very intelligent; others are dull. Some have normal bodies; others are disfigured and live in wheelchairs. A good actor plays his part to the very best of his ability within the boundaries of the character. In a similar sense, we are actors, playing roles which are often restricted by circumstances beyond our control. God only asks that we play the part to the best of our ability. Academy awards will be given later.

Thornton Wilder, the famous author, once remarked in speaking of the restrictions of any sort of art: "Every form is a restriction. . .but a restriction can be a challenge." Once the restrictions have been conquered, they become the servants of the artist. Acceptance of limitations can bring the power to transcend them.

Rising above restrictions is based upon attitude. Attitudes are formed throughout life but can be improved by conscious effort. Two people can look at the same situation and have entirely different outlooks. Napoleon, who seemingly had everything, said: "I have never known six happy days in my life." Helen Keller, who faced so many obstacles, remarked: "I have found life so beautiful." Our attitudes reflect what is in us, just as a spectrum reflects light. We see in our environment what we are inside. There is an old story told about seven men who walked through a field. The farmer saw only grass and fields. The astronomer observed the horizon and stars. The physician noticed the standing, stagnant water. The soldier studied how troops could be placed. The geologist saw the rocks and soil. The real estate broker decided how he would divide the land into lots. The poet observed the shadows, landscape, and the singing of birds. It was the same field, seen in seven various aspects. It's the same life, but each person interprets it differently according to what he is inside - his attitude.

> One ship drives east and another drives west
> With the selfsame winds that blow.
> "Tis the set of the sails
> And not the gales
> Which tells us the way to go.
> Ella Wheeler Wilcox

An alloy, like brass, is composed of at least two elements; but the combination is stronger than any of its separate parts. A person who is victorious over hardships is much like an alloy. His goals or desires in life are combined with his despair over circumstances over which he has no control. The blending of the two produces a strong individual who is an inspiration to other burdened souls. "He hath put a new song in my mouth, even praise unto our God: Many shall see it, and fear, and shall trust in the Lord" (Psalms 40:3). Although we cannot change Nature, we can change our natures. When we change ourselves, the world around us changes also.

I have made a collection of examples of people who have transcended adversity to enjoy a rich and full life: a man who lost his eyes and hands in a dynamite explosion and learned to read Braille with his tongue; a blind and epileptic boy who learned to ride a bicycle; a sixteen-inch man who turned his size into money; many physically disabled people who have overcome their misfortunes and have accomplished much more than most normal people. Physical handicaps, although more evident, are not the only ones which people must bear. Many with broken hearts have struggled just as hard as those previously mentioned and have been victorious. They have learned to build cathedrals out of ruins.

CLIMB 'TIL YOUR DREAM COMES TRUE

Often your tasks will be many,
And more than you think you can do -
Often the road will be rugged
And the hills insurmountable, too -
But always remember, the hills ahead
Are never as steep as they seem,
And with Faith in your heart start upward
And climb 'til you reach your dream.

Helen Steiner Rice

Learn To Help Others

It has been said that a person completely wrapped up in himself makes a small package. Let's face it. Most humans are self-centered creatures. To us, our troubles seem to be the most terrible ones in all the world. No one suffers as we do. Nothing can jolt us from our self-pity as quickly and effectively as when we lift our heads and look around us. My recovery has necessitated visits to a rehabilitation center. It only takes a few glances to make me humbly thank God that everything has turned out so well for me.

There are all sorts of troubles - some physical, some emotional, some spiritual. As a minister's wife, I constantly come in contact with people who have every burden imaginable. Being in such a position has been good for me; it has helped me with my sense of perspective by keeping my thoughts turned outward instead of inward upon my own petty problems. Sometimes when I'm feeling low, I only have to listen to another person's troubles to realize that I actually have no difficulties at all. We all need minds with windows instead of mirrors. An oriental proverb states: "I was without shoes, and I murmured, until I met a man without feet."

The Scriptures tell us to bear one another's burdens (Galatians 6:2). Also, "we then that are strong ought to bear the infirmities of the weak" (Romans 15:1). How do we become strong? By sitting at home and weeping over our own troubles? Of course not. We develop our spiritual muscles by helping another shoulder part of his load. Not only do we help our weak brother, but we will also return to our own tasks with greater strength. One of the most pleasant thoughts is the knowledge that we are needed and can add to the happiness of others. I agree with Albert Schweitzer's viewpoint: "I have always held firmly to the thought that each one of us can do a little to bring some portion of misery to an end." We cannot look for happiness. The only way to find true happiness is by bringing it to others, by expanding ourselves, and by investing a little of self in someone else. Sometimes others need only our presence and support, not advice. When a person's heart is truly heavy, we do more harm than good when we are flippantly cheerful. "As he that taketh away a garment in cold weather, and as vinegar upon nitre, so is he that singeth songs to an heavy heart" (Proverbs 25:20).

Helping others has a healing effect. Abraham Lincoln said, "to ease another's heartache is to forget one's own." How wise are the words of George Bernard Shaw: "The secret of being miserable is to have the leisure to bother about whether you are happy or not." After the emotional ordeal of seeing his master crucified, Peter got busy: "I go a fishing" (John 21:3). We would all do well to follow his example.

"Keep your fears to yourself but share your courage with others" (Robert Louis Stevenson).

Find the Good

The measure of mental health
is the disposition to find
good everywhere.
             Ralph Waldo Emerson

Notice that the heading of this section said "**Find** the good," not just **look** for the good. There **is** good in every burden if only we will take the trouble to find it. We read Romans 8:28: "And we know that all things work together for good to them that love God. . ." But we only window shop. We don't really buy the passage. We should have the confidence of Paul: "Wherefore, sirs, be of good cheer: for I believe God, that it shall be even as it was told me" (Acts 27:25). The same God who inspired the writing of Mark 16:16 also inspired Paul to write Romans 8:28. Why do we accept the first so readily and yet doubt the truthfulness of the second?

We should remember that it takes both the low and the high chords to make all the notes. In the same manner, it takes the low and high points of life to make a melody. We may not completely **understand** this principle during the low times, but we accept it in faith.

Monuments do not mark the only battlefields. The most significant battles have been fought and won in the hearts of the faithful, who may have been confused and discouraged but who have had enough faith to believe that somehow things would work out for the best and who have kept on trying in spite of their tears.

When we are heartbroken over the troubles which we face today, there is a tendency to retreat to former days which can be no more. Memories serve useful purposes: they are the bridges over which we pass yesterday to the uncertainties of tomorrow. Looking back turned Lot's wife to a pillar of salt, but our energy can be drained by constantly running back with the mind's eye to view scenes which can be no more - energy which is needed for the future. Like Paul, we must forget those things which are behind (Philippians 3:13) and reach to the future. Before the door of Christian maturity can be opened, we must close many others. It was Carl Sandburg who said that we must be big enough "to loosen your hands, let go and say good-by." There comes a time when bridges must be burned. We must put the past into the back of our minds, accept the present, and travel with faith into the future. "Thou shalt forget thy misery, and remember it as waters that pass away" (Job 11:16). Before we leave the site of the burned bridge it is best to sift through the ashes. There we will find precious nuggets of gold: **the lessons learned.** These we should tuck close to our hearts so they will never be lost, and turn our steps toward the future. Sometimes we are so discouraged that we think there is no future; we feel that we have come to the end of the road. For those who have experienced this sense of bewilderment, I would like to share with you one of my favorite poems by Helen Steiner Rice. Several dear friends sent collections of Mrs. Rice's poetry to me when I was hurt. This particular poem has been very special to me. It is now wrinkled and splattered with coffee, food stains, and many tears because I kept it under my pillow on the hospital bed where I could reach it easily for several months. A number of times each day I would pull it out and read it over and over.

THE END OF THE ROAD
IS BUT A BEND IN THE ROAD

When we feel we have nothing left to give
And we are sure that the "song had ended" -
When our day seems over and the shadows fall
And the darkness of night has descended,
Where can we go to find the strength
To valiantly keep on trying,
Where can we find the hand that will dry
The tears that the heart is crying -
There's but one place to go and that is to God

And, dropping all pretense and pride,
We can pour out our problems without restraint
And gain strength with Him at our side -
And together we stand at life's crossroads
And view what we think is the end,
But God has a much bigger vision
And He tells us it's ONLY A BEND -
For the road goes on and is smoother,
And the "pause in the song" is a "rest,"
And the part that's unsung and unfinished
Is the sweetest and richest and best -
So rest and relax and grow stronger,
LET GO and LET GOD share your load,
Your work is not finished or ended,
You've just come to "A BEND IN THE ROAD."
                                   Helen Steiner Rice

Without a doubt I can say that the part that's unsung and unfinished **has** been the sweetest and richest and best. Like anyone else, I have no idea what other bends in the road may lie ahead; and I'm so thankful that I don't know. But now I have accepted what I have intellectually known all my life: I'll never have to face any problem alone. "I the Lord. . .will hold thine hand" (Isaiah 42:6).

Suggestions for Class Use
Lesson Four

1. Has God ever expected humans to meet problems without fears and doubts? Why? Discuss the agony of Christ in the garden (Luke 22).
2. List several ways of expressing our fears and doubts in a manner that is acceptable to God.
3. What are the dangers involved when we bottle our emotions inside?
4. What are the three heavy burdens which most Christians carry upon their backs?
5. What is the best manner to handle previous troubles?
6. What can be done about the misfortunes of tomorrow?

7. Discuss the illustration concerning living in "day-tight" compartments and also the lesson learned from the hourglass.

8. When hardships actually strike, what are the three ways in which they can be met? Discuss each of them, trying to discover the best solution for each type of situation. (This question could best be handled by dividing the class into three smaller groups.)

9. When a problem cannot be met head-on and when patience in waiting for something better seems futile, we can only rise above the burden. What does this mean?

10. Are we the keys on a piano or are we the players? Are we thermometers or thermostats?

11. What is the meaning of **crisis**?

12. What is the meaning of the term **challenge of restrictions**? Give examples.

13. Discuss the story told about the different outlooks of the seven men who walked across a field. Relate this to a Christian's outlook on life.

14. How can a Christian be compared with an alloy?

15. If we can't change nature, what can we change?

16. How can helping another person bear his burden possibly make our load seem lighter?

17. According to Proverbs 25:20, how can false cheerfulness hinder rather than help the distressed?

18. Read Romans 8:28, Acts 27:25 and Mark 16:16 aloud in class and relate to the lesson.

19. What useful purpose do memories serve? What are their dangers? When they prevent our adapting to new situations, what is the best method of handling memories?

20. Elicit from the class members their own personal experiences in believing that they had come to the end of the road, only to find that the end was a bend.

21. Summarize the five suggestions for handling a problem when it actually comes: learn how to express emotions properly, carry only one day's burdens at a time, transcend troubles, learn to help others, and find

the good. Add others. Combine these methods with
the ones suggested in the previous chapter to help Christians lay the proper foundation.

5

The Cup of Petty Annoyances

"Father, sometimes I feel so frustrated. I truly want to be a faithful servant in Thy kingdom and engage in useful activities which will further Thy cause. How very much I want to develop a sweet, kind, loving disposition so others can see Christ living in me. My intentions are good, but so many trivial irritations arise each day. The children fight with one another. I worked so hard to wax the kitchen floor only to have Johnny run across it with his muddy shoes. Just as soon as I finish one meal and clean up the kitchen, it's time to turn around and begin another one. And the dirty clothes! They must multiply in the dirty clothes hampers because we don't even own that many. It seems that all I do is wash and put away clothes. When will the time come when I can do something of value in Thy kingdom?"

How convenient it would be if problems arrived wrapped in red paper with DANGER signs printed all over them! Then we would **know** to handle them with care and be extremely cautious lest we become trapped in some unfortunate circumstances. So many of the vexations that come our way, however, are wrapped in plain, brown paper with no indications of inherent danger. These are the ones that **bug** us the most. Perhaps it's because we steady ourselves for the big troubles, are aware of our weaknesses, and rely upon help from God to enable us to survive them. The little annoyances creep up from behind; we usually pay little attention to them and don't even bother God with these problems until we happen to glance backward and realize that we have been completely overwhelmed by such nuisances.

When God's people faced the seemingly impossible task of taking Jericho, they felt their weakness and relied completely upon His instructions. The walls fell with an overwhelming mightiness. The next town (Ai) seemed to pose no particular threat, but the Israelites were defeated (Joshua 6-8). Human nature has changed very little through the years.

We read Galatians 5:19-21 and pat ourselves on the back because **we're** not guilty of adultery, idolatry, witchcraft, murders, drunkenness and such like. Then we go on down to verses 22 and 23 and turn red. Let's face it. We're not exactly paragons of love, joy, peace, long-suffering, gentleness, goodness, faith, meekness, and temperance. We blush with shame over our lack of spiritual growth. We get so bogged down in daily living that we often feel we're just treading water and getting nowhere. With Thoreau we can say, "our lives are frittered away by detail."

The Problem Is An Old One

Thousands of years ago Confucious put his finger on our problem when he said: "Men do not stumble over mountains, but over molehills." An unknown sage once observed that the greatest cause of ulcers was mountain climbing over molehills. After all, a person is just about as big as the things which make him angry.

The Israelites prized their vineyards very highly and protecting them has been a major concern for centuries. Naturally the vines were sometimes trampled by large wild beasts or marauding nomads, but Solomon warned against the most insidious enemy of all—the sneaky little fox that stealthily crept in while no one was looking to feast upon the tender grapes (Song of Solomon 2:15).

We may not be in the grape business, but Solomon has a lesson in this passage especially applicable to Christian women. Into our charge has been entrusted the care not of vineyards but of homes. Just as the sly little foxes posed a menace to the Israelites, so do **little** vexations undermine our lives.

California has been losing some of its giant Sequoias in recent years. When Columbus first touched the new world, these plants were merely saplings. Through avalanches and earthquakes the mighty trees remained firm. Lightning had struck them many times. Do you know what has finally caused their destruction? Little carpenter ants have gnawed their way, little by little, through the protective bark to damage the inside.

You have probably heard the story concerning the man who had walked across this nation. Someone asked him about the greatest problem he had faced. Surprisingly, his reply was not the heat nor storms nor robbers. Instead, the greatest vexation he had encountered was the sand that kept getting into his shoes!

Several years ago it was necessary to have some grafting done in my mouth before my bridgework could be completed. A friend asked me what sort of ordeal it was. I replied that there was nothing to the grafting, but those hairpins at the back of my head nearly killed me when I had to sit with my head in a fixed position for so long. The pins felt as if they were coming through my head and out my eyeballs! As in so many other circumstances, it's the petty irritations that annoy us most.

The Solution

One of our astronauts who walked on the moon later admitted that the most difficult part of his life began when he returned to the earth. Earth problems were the ones that overwhelmed him. I've weathered some problems in this life, and I've also had my share of the little foxes about which Solomon gave his warnings. I'll have to be honest and confess that the little foxes have posed the greatest threat. I've thought about the matter a great deal and have gleaned two suggestions which may be of some benefit.

First, we should weed out the clutter in our lives. So many days we feel as if there must be a hundred hands reaching out to us, each demanding some of our time. Many, or most, of these causes may be very good ones; but one person can do just so much! It's small wonder that we're so short on patience. One of our well-known catalogs used to classify its merchandise as GOOD, BETTER or BEST. Baking cookies for a community project may be a **good** thing, but it could crowd out a **better** activity. School activities, scout troops, little league ballgames, clubs, and a dozen other demands on our time may be very honorable and worthwhile; but they can be quite harmful when they become too numerous, especially if they stunt our spiritual activities. It takes a lot of courage to get tough with ourselves and learn to resign or say "No" to worthwhile activities when they become oppressive.

Several years ago I planted some petunias in two flower boxes which my children had given me for Mother's Day. They looked so pretty that I thought a few more in each box would make them look even better. In my haste and ignorance, I planted too many. Alas, the flowers grew rapidly; but they were so crowded that their growth soon became stunted. The soil simply could not support that much life. There's also a limit as to how many activities **our** lives can adequately handle.

Second, get a change of perspective and realize that some trivial affairs are very important. Being happy is not dependent upon doing what we like, but liking what we do. If running a home is to be a happy experience, we must somehow see beyond the routine.

Occasionally it is helpful if we can get away from the daily grind to sort out priorities. Many of us suffer from spiritual nearsightedness. "He that lacketh these things (Christian graces) is blind, and cannot see afar off" (2 Peter 1:9). When we're lying on our stomachs in the grass on a spring day, a bug on a blade of grass can seem quite large. When we leave that area, however, and hike up the trail to the top of the mountain, we don't see that bug anymore. In fact, we don't even notice the grass; and the trees that once towered over us now seem quite small in comparison to the vastness of the world around us from our new point of view. When we're in the midst of spilled milk, dirty diapers, dishes stacked in the sink and all the other necessary parts of running a home and rearing a family, these annoyances can seem like real tribulations. From the top of the mountain, however, they're very insignificant.

Third graders aren't fed a diet of "Dick and Jane" in their readers anymore. One of their stories made quite an impression on me. Once there was a little boy who noticed that the windows in the house across the valley on the mountainside gleamed like real gold. Day by day he watched this phenomenon until he could stand it no longer. Even though the trip through snow down the side of his own mountain would be difficult, he decided to make his way to this house and find the gold. As the dawn broke, he looked once again. There were the gleaming windows, so the lad began the long journey. By the end of the day the youngster was weary, but he had finally reached his destination. Imagine his disappointment when he walked up to the house and found the windows were dark. Bewildered, he wept tears of frustration until he noticed that high on the opposite mountain was a cabin whose windows sparkled as gold. When the boy looked more closely, he discovered that it was **his own** cabin. It had not been gold, but the sun that had burnished the windows. From the opposite mountain his own humble home now seemed to have windows of gold. **We** have windows of gold in **our** own homes. How tragic it is that we often nearly have to lose them before we can realize how valuable and how important they are.

Specific Examples—I don't think I'm too different from the average Christian woman. So many of our problems are basically the same. Romans 12:1 admonishes Christians to present their bodies as living sacrifices, but do we have to be hacked into a hundred different pieces and spread out in so many different directions?

We all become weary of spending so much time preparing food that is gulped down in only a few minutes. It is our attitude that determines whether it is a chore or a blessing. Once I received a letter from a dear Christian friend who suffered from rheumatoid arthritis and couldn't walk a step. She told me that when she first became ill, she had a teenage son. One day her hands and feet were a little better; she made him a chocolate cake. She wrote, "I'll never forget how he ate that cake!" How often we grumble because we **have** to cook. So many would love to be **able** to cook. One Sunday I had cooked dinner ahead of time so I

could visit the nursing home after the church services. In
some way the bowl of Cool Whip was dropped on the floor
(right side up), and it exploded with the force of a hydrogen
bomb. That sticky mess went everywhere—all over the
table, on the light fixture, even on the ceiling. A big blob
landed on the dog's tail! He was going in circles trying to
lick it off. Before I could visit the "sick and elderly," I had to
scrub everything from ceiling to floor and even had to put
the dog in the bathtub. To say that I was vexed is putting
the matter mildly; I'm afraid I wasn't in a spiritual frame of
mind when I started out for my visits. It wasn't too long,
however, until my outlook changed. As I went from room to
room, my attitude began to soften. One woman was sitting
by the window, watching the rain and hoping that some of
her children would come that day. She seemed so lonely.
Another waited in complete darkness, for she had been
blind for years. All she could do, day after day, was just sit
there, tied in a chair, listening to sounds and hoping to hear
a familiar footstep. Another one rocked a doll, reliving
earlier days when she had held her own baby in her arms.
So many could not even enjoy the pleasure of sitting up.
Day after day, there was no change—just lying there and
looking at the ceiling and the four walls. It was only by the
grace of God that I had not been left as a vegetable when I
had been hurt. How quickly we forget all His blessings and
grumble over honest work! How many of those elderly
people would have gladly exchanged places with me that
day. How many would willingly have washed the floor and
ceiling if only they had been physically able to get down on
their hands and knees.

I've got a son who feels "uncomfortable" when he wears
shoes, so he frequently deposits them by the door when he
comes in the house. One day I felt particularly exasperated
as I nearly fell over some boots, and I'm afraid I unleashed
my fury. Ironically enough, that very same day the news
report featured one of the children who had been badly
deformed because his mother had been given a certain drug
before he was born. He was such a pitiful sight at age five
with no legs or arms—not even stubs. There was only a
trunk, a neck, and a head. Although it was evident that the

child had an alert mind, day in and day out he only existed in that stump of a body. I could not help feeling ashamed as I thought how gladly that mother would have exchanged places with me. Her boy had never thrown his messy shoes on the floor. Nor would he ever **clutter anything.** As I sat there repenting of my ingratitude, I could not help but remember all the children who daily sit in wheel chairs and wistfully watch others play. I don't suppose their mothers ever have to worry about tattered shoes being thrown on the floor.

Mothers, never feel that your children no longer need you just because they're growing older. Their needs are different, but they need you just the same. One day a thirteen-year-old boy came running into his mother's kitchen with the news that his little dog had just been run over. She ran outside and detected a slight heartbeat in the lifeless form of his pet. While the boy gathered his dog into his arms, the mother ran into the house for the car keys, and they raced to the office of the veterinarian. When they arrived, the last thread of life had left the little pet; and mother and son returned home. The boy insisted that it was his responsibility and he would take care of the burying himself. Through all this, he had never shed a tear. When he finished burying his dog, he went into his room and closed the door for about thirty minutes. The boy had taken his first steps into the responsibilities of manhood, and he needed the moral support of his mother that day just as much as he needed her the day he took his first baby steps.

One day I got the vacuum cleaner out to begin the usual weekly cleaning. In the process I thought about how hard I would work that day and how messed up things would be two days later, so I put the vacuum back into the closet, made myself a cup of coffee and just thought for a few minutes. I don't know much about motors, but I do know that they cannot run smoothly without oil. In a sense, mothers are to their homes what oil is to motors. The tasks may not seem very glamorous, but they're necessary if a home is to run smoothly.

"Dear God, when I become so exasperated with the strewn possessions of normal living, when I lose patience over performing so many routine tasks that are usually taken for granted, please give me the wisdom to see beyond these 'things' to the immortal souls placed in my charge. The purpose of life is living. Homes are to be havens from the demands of this world, not museums or showplaces. My children are not perfect (neither am I) but have to be trained. When I become so discouraged, help me stop and listen to the sounds of a healthy, happy family. Being the lubricating oil may not put me in the spotlight, but You know and You understand how necessary my role is. I had rather bask one day in the eternal light of Thy heavenly presence than briefly to enjoy being in the spotlight on this earth. Forgive me for my ingratitude. There was a time when I begged for the privilege of once again being able to care for my family. May I perform my daily tasks with cheerfulness, aware that I am helping to shape immortal souls. May I realize that I must first learn to be faithful in the little things before I can prove my worth in weightier responsibilities. We forget so soon. . ."

Suggestions for Class Use
Lesson Five

1. Why can petty irritations pose such a threat?
2. From chapters 6, 7 and 8 of Joshua discuss the taking of the cities of Jericho and Ai. Why was the taking of Ai so difficult?
3. Read Galatians 5:19-23 aloud in class. How do you measure up to the qualities in verses 22 and 23? How does a failure to meet these qualities differ from possessing the vices mentioned in verses 19 through 21?
4. How would you evaluate the statement made by Confucious: "Men do not stumble over mountains, but over molehills"?
5. Solomon warned the Israelites to watch for what little enemy? (Song of Solomon 2:15).
6. Sometimes little foxes (unless checked) can become big ones. What did Christ call Herod? (Luke 13:31,32).
7. What has recently caused the death of a number of California's giant Sequoias? Make the application to

daily life. Use other illustrations mentioned in your lesson and add personal ones of your own.

8. How can weeding some of the clutter out of our lives help us develop more patience in dealing with petty annoyances? List some unnecessary activities.

9. How would you evaluate the second suggestion: get a change of perspective and realize that some seemingly trivial affairs are very important?

10. A person is spiritually nearsighted if he lacks what things? (See 2 Peter 1:9).

11. How can getting away from the routine help a person place the affairs of life in a better perspective? Illustrate with the story concerning the windows of gold.

12. The author concluded the lesson with several personal experiences which helped her realize the importance of so many routine tasks. Either divide the class into smaller discussion groups or have each member list an example of her own on a slip of paper. Share the results with the entire class.

6

The Cup of Feeling Inadequate

"Father, I truly want to do so much more in Thy service, but it seems that I just don't know how. As long as I stay in the background and don't stick my neck out, I won't take so many chances on becoming embarrassed. If only I had more training, I could do more for Thee. Please forgive me, but I just don't think I can take an active part."

In a sense, this chapter is out of place in such a study. All the other chapters deal with problems with which many Christians must deal from time to time. The **problem** of feeling inadequate is actually not a burden to be borne but a blessing in disguise. If taken with the right attitude, a feeling of inadequacy can be the springboard to accomplishments unattainable by those who are self-satisfied and complacent. "Success or failure is caused more by mental attitude than by mental capacities." Having a feeling of inadequacy and not being aware of its worth is similar to the plight of someone who has been willed a million dollars and never even knows about the legacy.

Biblical Examples

A casual thumbing through the Scriptures shows numerous cases of people who felt that they were not capable of doing the task. In the third and fourth chapters of Exodus the reader becomes so exasperated with Moses as he fumbled through five excuses for not appearing before Pharaoh. This one who had once held such a favored position at the court felt so inferior in pleading the cause of the Israelites. **But,** he did it anyway and became the

powerful leader of God's people through forty difficult
years. One would hardly recognize the spineless Midianite
shepherd as the one who boldly stood before Pharaoh and
stubbornly defied this mighty ruler.

The Israelites felt vastly inferior to the Amorites. "The
people is greater and taller than we; the cities are great and
walled up to heaven" (Deuteronomy 1:28). Ten of the spies
who examined the promised land had a **grasshopper**
complex and felt totally inadequate to overtake the country
(Numbers 13:25-33). When the angel of the Lord asked
Gideon to fight the Midianites, he felt unfit as he said: "O
my Lord, wherewith shall I save Israel? behold my family is
poor in Manasseh, and I am least in my father's house"
(Judges 6:15). Many of Gideon's followers also felt afraid
and even returned home when given the choice (Judges
7:3). Barak had his misgivings about leading the Israelite
army and wanted Deborah to accompany him into battle
(Judges 4:8). The children of God were afraid when
confronted with the threats of Goliath (1 Samuel 17:24).
Turning over to the New Testament, we find that the man
with one talent was afraid and hid his talent in the earth
(Matthew 25:25). The fearful will even have a place in the
lake which burneth with fire and brimstone (Revelation
21:8).

Our Source of Strength

Feeling inadequate at times is not wrong; it is only
human. Failure to do something about it is the sin. No
person can properly elevate himself until he realizes his
only source of true strength. Paul said that when he was
weak, then he was strong (2 Corinthians 12:10). The same
writer declared in Philippians 4:13 that he could do all
things through Christ which strengthened him. In 4:19 Paul
affirmed his faith that "God shall supply all your need
according to his riches in glory by Christ Jesus." The
psalmist declared that the Lord was his strength in Psalm
19:14.

Secular Findings

Before we make the spiritual application, let's turn to the thoughts of some who make a study of human behavior. Freud discovered the subconscious and felt that the behavior pattern of a person is set during his first five or six years and is very difficult to change. There are others (Pavlov, Thorndike, Watson, Hall, and Meyer) who have used heredity and environment to explain behavior. Some even felt that behavior is strongly influenced by the chemical balance in a person's body.

Alfred Adler, a Viennese psychiatrist during the years before World War I, was a pioneer in a new field dealing with inferiority complexes. His findings, based upon studies of normal people, formed the foundation of his conclusions that a feeling of inferiority can either be a liability or an asset. The human behaviorists before Adler felt that heredity and environment were the two primary influences in a person's life. Adler added a third factor—**the reaction of an individual to these influences.** Since very little can be done to change either environment or heredity, the only realistic manner in which an individual can change his life is to change his opinion of himself.

In examining cadavers, Adler found that the body compensates for defects in one part of the body by making other organs even stronger. For example, when one kidney is removed, the other one is larger than normal. When one lung is weakened, the other lung becomes stronger. Not only does the body unconsciously compensate for weaknesses, there is also a psychological compensation. Those with handicaps often over-compensate for their deficiency and develop untapped strength. For example, when Adler tested the eyesight of artists in leading art schools, he found that over 70 percent had serious sight deficiencies. Through the years these people had made a special effort to see and notice, which, in turn, had improved their art. Demosthenes, who had great difficulty in speaking, recited before a mirror with pebbles in his mouth and did other work until he conquered his weakness and became the greatest orator of his age.

Examples—History books abound with examples of people who keenly felt their shortcomings in some area and were so determined to overcome them that they actually excelled far more than people who felt satisfied and had no desire to improve. Inadequacies can include those that are physical, temperamental, intellectual, circumstantial, or social. Just as "the north wind made the Vikings," so can adversities and feelings of inadequacies drive us to great heights. It was William James who said that our infirmities help us unexpectedly. In his essay on "Compensation" Ralph Waldo Emerson maintained that no man ever had a defect that was not somewhere made useful to him. He went on to elaborate that the world looks like a mathematical equation which will eventually balance itself.

Napoleon was a poor student in school. James Russell Lowell made unsatisfactory marks at Harvard. President Wilson had low grades at Princeton. Sir Isaac Newton began to study when he was beaten up by a bully who made better grades. Later Newton became one of the greatest mathematicians and philosophers of his time. Some attribute Leonardo da Vinci's success in so many fields to his feelings of inferiority over being an illegitimate child. Benjamin Franklin, who was born in poverty and only had two years of formal schooling, became a scientist, inventor, and statesman, replacing each liability with an asset. Abraham Lincoln was born with three strikes against him, but his desire to achieve was so great that he rose above his deficiencies to become one of the greatest presidents of this nation. Many of the **greats** had something wrong with their bodies—Keats, Stevenson, Pope, Kant, Byron, Chopin, Wagner, Bacon, Aristotle and others. Many believe that the desire to overcome deficiencies was the motivating drive behind these men. A one-legged man overcame his handicap so well that he ran the hundred yard dash in eleven seconds. Alfred Gerald Caplin, who lost his leg in a streetcar accident, couldn't be active so he drew cartoons. Today we know him as Al Capp, the originator of Li'l Abner. Charles Atlas, a 97 pound runt, became the world's most perfectly developed man. Glen Cunningham had wanted to break the record for running but was paralyzed from his waist down early in life in a schoolhouse fire. He

had his father tie his hands to the plow handle and let the
mule drag his feet around the field to regain his strength.
At the age of 25 he broke the world's record for the mile
run. Fannie Crosby, blinded when only 6 years old, wrote
more than 6000 hymns.

Now let's put it all together. Why do we act the way we
do? We're free moral agents but much goes into our
makeup. The subconscious part of our minds reacts
according to the information which is fed to it. We develop
lifestyles to meet the goals which we have subconsciously
set for ourselves. Failure can be attributed to feelings of
inferiority but so can success. The same situation can
produce different reactions in different people, making
saints of some and sinners of others. The average person
often becomes discouraged and quits trying when faced by
an obstacle. Some try to hide behind shyness, timidity, or
bragging. Others assume a sour grapes attitude. A few
escape into a daydream or fantasy world, denying reality
because it is too painful. The ones with criminal tendencies
have neurotic reactions. The truly successful person is
stimulated by the adversity, whatever it might be, to
overcome it and become even more successful than before.
It is the individual's **reaction** to whatever he feels is lacking
in his life that determines whether he will be dragged down
into the mire or will rise to great heights. If people react
positively, then their subconscious prods them to prove to
the world that they are not what they feared the most.
There are a number of ways to compensate. One can
substitute or sublimate, which often leads to better things,
producing understanding and sympathy; he can use the
defect to an advantage; he can train the defective part to
work even better than normal; he can use his whole being
to compensate for all his weaknesses. Being a success or
failure is ultimately up to the individual.

Spiritual Application

All these secular findings would be of little significance
unless we are able to apply them to the betterment of our
spiritual lives. Suppose a Christian is very hesitant about
talking with others concerning religious matters. If that

deficiency prods him in the right manner, it will goad him into taking that first step, however small and seemingly insignificant. It will cause him to study and do all he can to learn how to improve his methods. The same principle holds true concerning the teaching of the Bible class. If a person really wants to teach but feels all thumbs, he will sit in on other classes to observe teachers; he will attend workshops; he will read method books; most of all, he will become a serious student of God's Word so he can teach it to others. Men who truly want to be leaders and take a public part in the worship serivce will make that a consuming passion in their lives. God has delegated woman to a place of submission; but, if she really wants to serve her Master, she will find suitable ways of doing so and will develop all her potentialities.

The source of divine power is available to the Christian through the Word. "Be strong and of a good courage, fear not, nor be afraid of them: for the Lord thy God, he it is that doth go with thee; he will not fail thee, nor forsake thee" (Deuteronomy 31:6).

If a Christian feels inadequate in one area, there is always another door open to him. This is called sublimation, or substitution. If, after an honest effort, he feels that the public roles are impossible for him, he can sublimate, or substitute, and channel his energies into a field that may be less spectacular but just as useful.

Most of the work in the kingdom of the Lord is done by average people who are faithful to the task.

> The heights by great men reached and kept
> Were not attained by sudden flight.
> But they, while their companions slept,
> were toiling upward in the night.
>   Anonymous

"Genius is not spontaneous combustion. It is a trail of sparks from a grindstone."

With Edward Everett Hale we can voice his sentiments:

I am only one,
But still I am one.
I cannot do everything,
But still I can do something.
And because I cannot do everything
I will not refuse to do the something that I can do.

"God, please forgive my lack of faith. Help me realize that the only way I can be of more service in Thy kingdom is by trying. Of course I'll make mistakes. There will be times when I will feel like a complete failure, but I want to serve Thee so badly that I am determined to overcome my weakness and make it my strength. When I become discouraged, please help me to keep on trying until my spiritually weak muscles are stronger than any others."

Suggestions for Class Use
Lesson Six

1. How can a feeling of inadequacy be a blessing in disguise?
2. Assign different class members the following people to report upon, discussing the inferior feelings of these characters: (1) Moses (Exodus 3 and 4) (2) the Israelites (Deuteronomy 1:21-33) (3) ten of the spies (Numbers 13:25-33) (4) Gideon (Judges 6:15) (5) Gideon's followers (Judges 7:3) (6) Barak (Judges 4:8) (7) Children of Israel meeting Goliath (1 Samuel 17:24) (8) the man with one talent (Matthew 25:25).
3. What is our only true source of strength? (See Philippians 4:13 and 19.) How could Paul be strong when he was weak? (See 2 Corinthians 12:10.)
4. A number of men have studied human behavior. Most of their theories explained man's actions in terms of environment and heredity. What third factor did Alfred Adler add? (A) What did Adler find when he examined dead bodies? (B) What other sort of compensations did he find?
5. William James said that our infirmities help us unexpectedly. What did he mean? Do you agree?

6. Your lesson listed a number of examples of people who were prodded to even greater successes by inadequacies which they felt very keenly. Discuss those that interest you.

7. How can both failure and success be attributed to feelings of inferiority? What are some of the vastly different reactions which people may make to the same situation?

8. What are some ways we can compensate for inadequacies?

9. Divide the class into two or three smaller groups to discuss the application of the principles involved in this lesson to the spiritual lives of Christians.

10. Instead of genius, how are most worthwhile things accomplished?

11. Since it is a personal matter, have each member write on a slip of paper what he considers to be his greatest inadequacy in the Lord's service and what he plans to do to overcome it. Elicit a commitment from each.

7

The Cup of Unjust Criticism

"Oh dear God, their remarks hurt so very deeply. I expect criticism from those of the world, but the words of my own brethren can stab my heart so deeply. How can I have the right attitude toward my fellow-Christians when they have been so unfair to me?"

Benjamin Franklin once remarked that only two things in life are certain: death and taxes, but he forgot criticism. Unless one draws into a shell and isolates himself from society, criticism at one time or another is almost inevitable. Nothing else hurts quite so deeply. With David we can say, "Yea, mine own familiar friend, in whom I trusted, which did eat of my bread, hath lifted up his heel against me" (Psalms 41:9). David voiced this same type of hurt in Psalm 55:12-14.

If it is any consolation, bickering among God's people has been going on since man first appeared on this earth. Cain started it all (Genesis 4). Lot had his differences with his Uncle Abraham (Genesis 13). Sarai and Hagar differed (Genesis 16:1-6). Jacob and Esau had their ups and downs (Genesis 25:27-34; 27:41-45). Joseph's dreams could have sparked the jealousy which his brethren displayed toward him (Genesis 37:2-36). Aaron and Miriam were jealous of Moses (Numbers 12:1,2). Even though the Law prohibited avenging or bearing grudges against brethren (Leviticus 19:18), the practice continued anyway. The Israelites griped about the bitter water (Exodus 15:23,24) and lack of food (Exodus 16:2,3). In Numbers 14:26-35 they were told that they would die in the wilderness because of their murmurings; the fiery serpents got many of them

(Numbers 21:6). Later the people of Judah and Israel disputed over such a trivial thing as who would bring David back over the Jordan (2 Samuel 19:11-15, 41-43).

The New Testament continues the same story. Laborers in the vineyard murmured over wages (Matthew 20:1-15). The disciples didn't like the wasting of money by pouring ointment on Christ's feet (Mark 14:5). The scribes and Pharisees murmured against the disciples and Jesus because they ate with publicans and sinners (Luke 15:2). Martha complained because Mary wouldn't help her prepare a meal (Luke 10:40). The elder brother murmured against the prodigal son (Luke 15:11-32). Christ received criticism for eating with Zacchaeus (Luke 19:1-9). The Grecians murmured against the Jews because some widows were neglected (Acts 6:1). There was contention between Paul and Barnabas over Silas and Mark (Acts 15:39,40). So you see, bickering is nothing new. So many Christians have the same philosophy as Jonah: "I do well to be angry" (Jonah 4:9). How wearisome our attitude must be to God! Have you ever noticed the first part of the admonition in Romans 12:18: "**If it be possible**, as much as lieth in you, live peaceably with all men"? The parables of the tares and the dragnet (Matthew 13) teach that the Lord realizes that there are both good and bad in the church, and He will leave it that way until judgment.

The realization that brethren have been murmuring against one another since the early pages of history may help us gain our sense of perspective, but it does not relieve us of responsibility. Loving God with all our beings may be the **greatest** commandment (Mark 12:30); but the most **difficult** one is found in Matthew 5:44, in which we are told to love those who treat us unfairly. Love of the brotherhood is stressed in John 13:35, 1 John 4:21, and 1 Peter 2:17. Christ, our supreme example in everything (1 Peter 2:21-24), was able to forgive those who had wronged Him (Luke 23:34), even when they were not penitent and did not ask for forgiveness.

In this study let us not overlook one very important point: **sometimes we deserve and need the criticism which we receive.** "He that hateth reproof shall die" (Proverbs 15:10). Before passing off the charges too lightly, we should always try to examine them objectively, realizing that we all do wrong at one time or another and that it is quite possible that we are guilty of a fault which we had never realized since we frequently do not see ourselves as others see us. "A man should never be ashamed to say he has been in the wrong, which is but saying in other words that he is wiser today than he was yesterday" (Alexander Pope).

Why Some Criticize

"A hammer is the only knocker
that does any good."

Since we've already considered the fact that some criticism is justified and is profitable if given and received in a Christian manner, let's now center our attention on the subject of **unjust** criticism—**unmerited** faultfinding.

First of all, we should honestly try to understand the backgrounds and problems of those who usually criticize the most. "The only mental exercise some ever get is jumping at conclusions." Even though the offender may be rude and completely out of place, forgiveness is easier if we know something about the forces which motivate such behavior. With Francis of Assisi we can voice, "Lord grant that I may seek more to understand than to be understood." If we could only see the road which the critic has traveled and could feel the rocks in his pathway, then perhaps we could better understand his reactions.

When a person constantly finds fault with others, the cause usually lies within. William Blake said, "As a man is, so he sees." Studies conducted by research groups at universities have shown that the typical faultfinder has a defective image of himself. Confucius said, "An angry man is always full of poison" but anyone ought to be able to figure that one out. The **only** way in which some people can feel important is by pulling others down. This is a very poor manner by which one can increase his self-esteem; but some have such an unhealthy image of themselves that faultfinding has become a habit, a way of life with them, an addiction (such as alcohol, nicotine, and drugs). Someone observed that we have all known people who are so intent on having their own way that they will tear up the world to have a stool to sit on. They are so frustrated with themselves that any innocent bystander can be the object of their aggression. We are admonished in Matthew 19:19 to love our neighbors as ourselves. How can a person properly love another when he actually hates himself?

Second, some who criticize are outwardly the most self-righteous. They fail to realize how many wrongs they have committed and feel no need of forgiveness for themselves. Naturally, such people can have little compassion for the mistakes of others. Christ said, "To whom little if forgiven, the same loveth little" (Luke 7:47). A truly penitent sinner who is grateful for the forgiveness of his wrongs is not likely to dwell upon the shortcomings of another person.

Third, others have never learned to keep their mouths shut. Since they rattle constantly, the law of averages is bound to catch up with them eventually; and they will say unkind remarks about people simply because they speak without thinking and have never bothered to find the facts. The ones who talk the most usually have the least to say. "Seest thou a man that is hasty in his words? there is more hope of a fool than of him" (Proverbs 29:20). Someone has said that great talkers are like leaky vessels; everything runs out of them. It was a very wise Abraham Lincoln who remarked: "He has the right to criticize who has the heart to help."

Why Criticism Hurts So Deeply

Anyone who has ever been the object of a critic's venom knows how deep the wounds can be. The Scriptures refer to the tongue as a sharp razor (Psalms 52:2), as a sword and arrows (Psalms 64:3), as serpents and adders' poison (Psalms 140:3). Proverbs 18:8 tells us that the words of a talebearer are as wounds and go down into the innermost parts of the belly. Any victim can testify that these phrases are not exaggerations.

Since criticism is a direct attack upon one's self-esteem, it is only natural that it should hurt. Some people apparently shrug off criticism with little trouble. They are able to do this because they have built thick protective shells around themselves. This practice has its advantages but also some significant disadvantages. When a heart has become so calloused that it does not feel hurt, it is also impenetrable by love and affection. To expose one's heart to love is to make it vulnerable. Going through life keeping others at arm's length is really not living. The price we pay for such protection is loneliness, isolation, and insensitivity to both good and bad. Most of us would not want to go along with the Buddhist philosophy: "Make thou, in all the world, nothing dear to thee." Common sense tells us that we need an epidermis to shield us from everyday slights and injustices, but we do **not** need tough shells.

Ways to Handle Unjust Criticism

(1) **Be rational.** To be criticized does not mean that you are a failure. No one kicks a dead dog. Earlier we discussed the importance of honestly examining the complaints to correct unrealized faults. When you have done this and feel that the criticism **is** unjust, accept the fact that busy, active people are the ones who are criticized, not the mousy ones who cringe in the corner all the time lest they offend someone. Do not expect everyone to love and admire you. All did not adore Christ. It is better to suffer for doing right than for doing wrong (1 Peter 3:16,17).

"Little minds are hurt by little things; great minds are aware of them but not bothered." Sometimes it is best to put up an umbrella and let the rain drain off instead of running down our backs.

(2) **Act instead of reacting.** Most of us **react** instinctively to the manner in which others treat us. It is more like a conditioned reflex. Instead of reacting, be master of the situation and plan your action. Don't allow others to decide how you're going to act. Make your own game plan.

(3) **Bite your tongue.** Milton said, "He who reigns within himself, and rules passions, desires and fears, is more than a king." A less eloquent writer observed: "Many things are opened by mistake but none so frequently as one's mouth," but he had the same idea as Milton. When we are hurt by someone, the natural instinct is to lash back; but it takes a

big person to walk away from a fight. "Heat not a furnace
for your foe so hot that it do singe yourself" (Shakespeare).
Allowing time to elapse before speaking is a mature Christian trait and must be cultivated. Ecclesiastes 3:7 states
that there is a time to keep silence and a time to speak. "A
fool uttereth all his mind: but a wise man keepeth it till
afterward" (Proverbs 29:11). Thomas Jefferson said:
"When angry, count ten before you speak; if very angry, an
hundred." To ignore anger is wrong because the wound
festers, but it is best to say the right words. "Let your
speech be alway with grace, seasoned with salt" (Colossians
4:6). Sometimes it's difficult to find the salt shaker when
we're so mad and upset. Solomon said: "He that refraineth
his lips is wise" (Proverbs 10:19). Once words are spoken,
they can be reclaimed just about as easily as feathers in the
wind. As long as the thoughts are in our minds, they are
ours. It is not so with spoken words. In Ecclesiastes 10:20
the writer warns against speaking slanderous words even
in one's bedchamber because "a bird of the air shall carry
the voice, and that which hath wings shall tell the matter."

Incidentally, instead of putting a filter on our mouths,
sometimes it is better to pour a little chlorine into our
hearts so we can be mature enough not to be offended too
easily. Love is not easily provoked (1 Corinthians 13:5). It
was Spurgeon who said, "What lies in the well of the heart
will come up in the bucket of speech."

(4) **Learn to forgive.** A key to good mental health is the
ability to handle hostile feelings. We don't forgive just to
obey God's commands. We forgive to be happy because we
are the ones who gain the most. Naturally we can't be
forgiving toward others unless we can be forgiving toward
ourselves. Some harbor grudges, roasting them over coals
of bitterness and self-pity until they have appetites for little
else.

Christ on the cross is the supreme example of forgiveness
(Luke 23:34). The Scriptures abound with commands to
forgive our fellowman. "Whosoever shall smite thee on thy
right cheek, turn to him the other also" (Matthew 5:39).
"Forbearing one another, and forgiving one another, if any
man have a quarrel against any: even as Christ forgave you,
so also do ye" (Colossians 3:13). If we don't forgive others,

neither will God forgive our wrongs (Matthew 6:15); and we are **all** sinners (1 John 1:8). "He who cannot forgive others breaks the bridge over which he must pass himself" (George Herbert). The parable of the unmerciful servant in chapter 18 of Matthew teaches the necessity of forgiveness if we hope to be forgiven.

Forgiveness is the epitome of love and is impossible without it. Anyone can love those who are nice to him. Loving those who have wronged him is a different matter. When we forgive, we forget because remembered forgiveness re-infects the wound. We should treat forgiveness like a canceled note: tear it up and burn it. Resentment comes from two Latin words ("re" meaning back and "sentire" meaning to feel). It is reliving or refeeling previous emotions. A wound must be thoroughly cleansed of resentment if it is to heal properly. In reality, resentment hurts the one who feels it.

"Forgiveness is the fragrance of the violet on the heel of the one who crushed it."

The following story illustrates forgiveness in action. Once a famous French portrait and landscape artist sent for a doctor to come to his house for an emergency. When the doctor arrived, he found that he had been called to set a dog's broken leg. When he had finished, the painter offered to pay; but the doctor asked him to come by the office the next week. When the painter arrived, the doctor took him to a room in the back and showed him a piece of furniture, a can of white paint and a cheap brush with the instructions to paint for the repayment of the bill. The painter knew that the doctor was trying to humiliate him, but he agreed to do the task if he could come and go through the back door to work on the project. Three weeks later he called the doctor in. On the piece of furniture he had painted a beautiful landscape. The doctor, in humiliation, told the painter, "I'm not the man you are."

When a person who has hurt us comes in humble penitence, begging forgiveness for his wrongs, the proper feelings on our part are not too difficult to evoke. When we have been hurt so deeply and the one who offended us is either indifferent or refuses to admit his transgressions, we still must forgive. (Note the example of Christ on the cross.)

We forgive others, not for what they are, but for what **we** are. And we are not paragons of self-righteous mercy who sit high and mighty on our thrones, charitably bestowing our forgiveness upon those who have hurt us much as a king grants pardon to his lowly subjects. In effect we are saying, "You should be thankful that you offended someone as godly as I am because others would not be so magnanimous."

Sometimes the hurt is so deep that all our rational powers will not—**cannot**—call forth complete forgiveness. Oh, we may intellectually forgive with the part which we can control; but sometimes the hurt is so very deep that the conscious part of our minds simply cannot penetrate the core of our beings—that part which reacts instinctively instead of reasoning. Quite often "reflective hurt" lies deep within not because someone has wronged **us** but one of our loved ones. Forgiveness in such an instance is a supreme test of our true Christianity. Although we may forgive with our rational powers, the injured part of our beings, down deep inside, simply will not surrender. It is at a time such as this (when we want to forgive but cannot) that we must cast ourselves upon the grace of God, begging for His help in creating within us a new heart and renewing a right spirit (Psalm 51:10). When we reach the nadir of our own ability and throw ourselves at the feet of God for His mercy, realizing that we are sinners just as much as the one who has wronged us or our loved ones because **we** are unable to forgive, we can achieve previously unattainable strength. Forgiveness in such an instance is a crowning achievement of Christianity. Our human natures stand as roadblocks in doing what our minds have been conditioned to do through His Word. When we reach the point that we realize that the spirit is willing but the flesh is weak (Matthew 26:41), we can cry unto God: "Father, I want to forgive but I can't. Please help me." Then we achieve real strength because we know that forgiveness does not come entirely through our own will or might but because we are aware of our inadequacies and throw ourselves at the mercy of God. "For when I am weak, then am I strong" (2 Corinthians 12:10).

(5) **Smother your critic with kindness.** "When the door squeaks, use a little oil" is just another way of expressing

Paul's philosophy concerning the treatment of one's enemies in Romans 12:14-21 in which he tells us to feed and clothe them. Instead of lashing back with unkind words and actions, try going out of your way to be nice to the person who has mistreated you. Such action usually takes the wind out of his sails and the venom out of his bite, in addition to heaping coals of fire on his head! Since it is human nature to respond in the same manner in which one has been treated, kindess makes it extremely difficult for the offender to continue his attacks. Years ago Alexander Campbell rightly observed: "To conquer an enemy is to convert him into a friend." Peter said: "Be courteous: not rendering evil for evil, or railing for railing: but contrariwise blessing" (1 Peter 3:8,9).

> He drew a circle that shut me out,
> Heretic, rebel, a thing to flout.
> But love and I had the wit to win;
> We drew a circle that took him in.
>   Edwin Markham

(6) **Should the matter be discussed?** When a person who has been criticized unjustly has allowed a "cooling off" time to elapse in which he has thought about the matter, trying to understand both his own reactions and the motives of his critic; when he has searched God's Word and has diligently prayed over the matter; when he has vented his feelings to a close, understanding Christian friend; when he has tried to befriend his enemy; he then faces the decision of whether to discuss the matter openly with his offender or not. There is no pat answer and each individual must use his own judgment. Frequently it is best to sit down with such a person in an open discussion to clear the air. "Therefore if thou bring thy gift to the altar, and there rememberest that thy brother hath ought against thee; leave there thy gift before the altar, and go thy way; first be reconciled to thy brother, and then come and offer thy gift" (Matthew 5:23,24). "Moreover if thy brother shall trespass against thee, go and tell him his fault between thee and him alone: if he shall hear thee, thou hast gained thy brother" (Matthew 18:15). If this can be done in a Christian manner, it can often

do wonders in cleansing the wound of all infection so it can heal properly. To say, "I don't completely understand why I have offended you; but, since I have, I want to offer my apologies" puts the critic on the defensive. Openly admit that you have been hurt. "This tear which you caused me to shed is yours. I place it at your feet" (Victor Hugo).

How sad it is that there are some brethren with whom it may be best not to discuss the matter since they're completely unreasonable. Sometimes it is wise just to let the matter drop. The offended one has to be the one to decide. Talk it over with God and do what you think is expedient.

When brethren cannot live together without friction, we have a biblical example of the best course of action. Paul and Barnabas could not agree on the advisability of taking Mark with them on a missionary journey so the two parted their ways (Acts 15:37-40). If, after all honest efforts have failed and brethren still cannot work together in love and harmony, sometimes it is best (both for the Lord's cause and their own welfare) that they come in contact with one another as little as possible.

(7) **Try sublimation.** When all other solutions for this problem fail, sublimation may be helpful. Sublimation means "out of this world." In chemistry some solids can be sublimated. When they are heated, they change into a gaseous state without becoming liquid. Such solids become sublime or of a higher order than their original state. Instead of working off frustration with attacks against the critic or against innocent people, it would be better to throw one's energies into an unrelated situation, accomplishing something that is socially and spiritually acceptable and satisfying. Do something to further the Lord's kingdom and help others; leave the rest to God. As David said of Shimei: "The Lord will requite me good for his cursing this day" (2 Samuel 16:12).

Suggestions for Class Use
Lesson Seven

1. There are two types of criticism. One is the kind that is justified and from which we can profit. The other is

unmerited and cruel. Discuss the differences in the
two and what our reactions should be to teach type.

2. In Psalms 41:9 David spoke of his friend who had
"lifted up his heel" against him. Discuss people in
David's life who would come under this category.
David's counselor, Ahithophel (2 Samuel 15:12),
turned against the King. Reconstruct the story of this
treason after reading 2 Samuel 17:1-4. For a better
understanding of Ahithophel's motives, discover
whose grandfather he was by reading 2 Samuel 11:3
and 23:34. Do you think this relationship could have
had any effect on his actions? How did David react to
the cursing of Shimei? (See Samuel 16:12.)

3. For a brief discussion assign different class members
the Scriptures mentioned in the first part of the lesson
concerning the bickering among God's people through
the years. Are people today basically any different?

4. Mark 12:30 gives the greatest commandment. What is
perhaps the most **difficult** one? (See Matthew 5:44.)
Why is it so difficult?

5. What is stressed in these passages: John 13:35, 1 John
4:21 and 1 Peter 2:17?

6. How was Christ our supreme example in forgiveness?
(See Luke 23:34 and 1 Peter 2:21-24.) What had He
taught in Matthew 5:38-45 concerning the treatment
of enemies?

7. The chronic faultfinder usually has what sort of image
of himself? How can constantly finding fault with
others give such a person a false feeling of superiority?

8. How can failure to have a healthy respect and
acceptance of ourselves influence our feelings toward
our neighbors? (See Matthew 19:19.)

9. Why does a self-righteous person have difficulty in
accepting the shortcomings of others? (See Luke 7:47.)

10. When a person talks **all** the time, by the law of
averages he will make some unjust criticisms. Why?

11. Use these Scriptures in describing how deeply words
can hurt: Psalms 52:2; Psalms 64:3; Psalms 140:3;
Proverbs 18:8.

12. People who are seemingly unaffected by criticism
have developed calloused hearts. Although this may

protect one from hurts, it also deprives him of much love and the beautiful things of life. Do you agree or disagree. Why?

13. Divide the class into seven smaller groups to discuss these suggestions for handling unjust criticism: (1) be rational, (2) act instead of reacting, (3) bite your tongue, (4) learn to forgive, (5) smother your critic with kindness, (6) discuss the matter with the critic in a Christian manner, (7) try sublimation.

14. Ephesians 4:26 states: "Be ye angry, and sin not." How can one be angry and not sin?

15. Make a black dot about the size of a dime on a sheet of white poster paper. Hold it in front of the class. What does nearly everyone notice? What about all that white space? Isn't it human nature to notice the bad?

16. Sometimes criticism results from misunderstanding the facts and even the motives of others. Illustrate this point by the story of David's servants and the Ammonites (2 Samuel 10:1-6).

17. John 13:35 admonishes the followers of Christ to love one another as a mark of discipleship. Romans 12:18 states: "If it be **possible**, as much as lieth in you, live peaceably with all men." Why is it impossible to live peaceably with some?

18. As time permits, read and study these passages from Proverbs concerning the proper use of the tongue: 10:19; 16:23; 25:11; 15:1; 14:29; 16:32; 19:11; 29:20; 15:23; 29:11; 25:15; 17:27,28; 16:21; 11:12; 25:21,22. Other passages also enrich our understanding: Ecclesiastes 12:10; Ecclesiastes 3:7 and 10:12; James 1:19; 1 Peter 3:10; Romans 12:16-21.

8
The Cup of Indifference

 The problem of indifference may not seem as serious as some of the other situations which we usually term "problems" (sickness, death, etc.), but it hangs like a millstone around the neck of each congregation of the Lord's people. If the church could be rid of indifference, she could take the world for Christ in just a few years in addition to saving many of her members from damnation.

Baptism is essential for salvation, but it only puts one on the right road. We must be faithful unto death to receive a crown of life (Revelation 2:10). Steadfastness in continuing in His service is taught in a number of passages. John 15:1-7 stresses the importance of **abiding** (remaining) in Christ just as the branch must abide in the vine to sustain life. "Be ye stedfast, unmoveable, always abounding in the work of the Lord. . ." (1 Corinthians 15:58).

In trying to analyze the problem of indifference, it seems that there are three groups of Christians affected: (1) those who are indifferent and don't care, (2) those who are unaware of their indifference even though their actions may be correct, (3) those who worry needlessly due to an inadequate understanding of spirituality.

Those Who Don't Care
The only change that takes place in some who are baptized is the fact that they enter baptism dry and come up wet. Since there was never any real conversion or change of mind, it is only natural that the plant withers since there were not any real roots anyway. Such people don't leave the faith; they were never really in it in the first

place. They did not faithfully attend the services of the Church to receive nourishment, nor did they ever do any serious Bible study at home. The parable of the soils (Matthew 13) emphasizes the sad fact that some of the seed would fall into stony places and be received with joy but would soon wither because the plants have no roots. Even a house will decay and fall down due to slothfulness and idleness of the hands (Ecclesiastes 10:18). Paul warned the Christians at Ephesus to guard against walking as other Gentiles walk, "Having the understanding darkened, being alienated from the life of God through the ignorance that is in them, because of the blindness of their heart; Who **being past feeling** have given themselves over unto lasciviousness" (Ephesians 4:18,19). Only the Word of God can save a person and keep him saved. The only hope for such people is additional teaching. Sometimes perhaps they, like Peter, will remember the Word of the Lord and repent (Luke 22:61).

Those Who Are Unaware

Isn't it tragic that some Christians attend every service of the Church, give of their means, go through most of the outward forms and yet have hearts as hard as stone! They do all the right things for the wrong reasons and display the same attitude of the priests who were rebuked by Malachi because they felt that the offering of sacrifices was such a weariness (Malachi 1:13). The counterparts of such people would be the scribes and Pharisees of Christ's day, whose attitudes were denounced in verses 23-36 of chapter 23 of Matthew. They paid their tithes but left other important things undone. Our Lord spoke very plainly of their hypocrisy when He said: "Ye blind guides, which strain at a gnat, and swallow a camel. . .ye make clean the outside of the cup and of the platter, but within they are full of extortion and excess. . .ye are like unto whited sepulchres, which indeed appear beautiful outward, but are within full of dead men's bones, and of all uncleanness. Even so ye also outwardly appear righteous unto men, but within ye are full of hypocrisy and iniquity." It seems that these people made their appearances quite frequently throughout the pages of the Gospels as they tried to hinder Jesus in His work. It was a Pharisee who thanked God that he was not as the lowly publican (Luke 18:9-14) in the parable which Christ spoke "unto certain which trusted in themselves that they were righteous, and despised others." The outward form is necessary, but it is not enough.

Although the Christians at Ephesus had many good works to their credit, they were chided because they had left their first love. John, through inspiration, admonished them to remember, repent, and do the first works (Revelation 2:4,5). The church at Laodicea had the same problem as many congregations today. It was filled with lukewarm members who were neither hot nor cold, thus producing a sickening condition (Revelation 3:15-22).

Peter gave Christians a formula for making their calling and election sure: ". . .for if ye do **these things**, ye shall never fall" (2 Peter 1:10). What things? The writer is referring to the Christian graces mentioned in verses 5-7 of the same chapter: faith, virtue, knowledge, temperance, patience, godliness, brotherly kindness, charity. "For **if** these things be in you, and abound, they make you that ye shall neither be barren nor unfruitful in the knowledge of our Lord Jesus Christ" (verse 8). How wise Peter was when he said we should remember the things which we already know (verse 12). Paul gave the same type of admonition in the book of Hebrews. "Therefore we ought to give the more earnest heed to the things which we have heard, lest at any time we **should let them slip**" (Hebrews 2:1).

The older brother in the parable of the lost son in Luke 15 is an example of negative goodness. How many indifferent Christians could make essentially the same statement as this brother: "Lo, these many years I do serve thee, neither transgressed I at any time thy commandment" (Luke 15:29). But his heart was hardened due to his rotten attitude! Instead of rejoicing over the return of his younger brother, who had repented of his wrongs, this one would not even come into the house. The Scriptures leave him standing outside pouting.

Once I noticed that the grass on the spot where I always parked the car was dead. I had not sprayed chemicals on it, nor had I set fire to it. It had been a gradual process in which the presence of the car had simply kept the blades

from receiving the life-giving rays of the sun. How similar is
this to the spiritual death of a Christian. We receive our
strength from the Lord. Like the grass, we may have that
source of strength all around us; but, if we allow something
(pride, arrogance, self-sufficiency) to cover and harden our
hearts, the sun's rays cannot reach us even though we are
in the midst of them all the time through regular church
attendance and other outward forms. Whenever we ask,
"How much do I **have** to do?" instead of "How much **can** I
do?" the grass is beginning to wither. "Whatsoever ye do,
do it heartily" (Colossians 3:23).

Those Who Worry Needlessly

Whereas some Christians are spiritually indifferent and
seem to be unaware that something is lacking, there are
others who are overly concerned. They study regularly,
attend all the services, do many good works, and have
tender hearts that are open to God's Word. No doubt their
anxiety is due to a lack of understanding of the meaning of
spirituality.

We are humans and have human emotions. All of us have
our emotional highs and lows. There are times when we feel
very close to God with tears in our eyes during worship
services. There are many other periods of worship when we
do not experience this same feeling. This should cause no
concern to the faithful child of God whose heart has not
been hardened and who has the right attitude. Sometimes
we think we should **feel** good rather than **be** good.

Our faith should be based upon the Word of God and His
promises rather than our emotions for these reasons:

(1) God is "not far from every one of us" (Acts 17:27). He
is everywhere (Psalms 139). It's just that we can't
always seem to find Him among all the clutter in
our lives. "Draw nigh to God, and he will draw nigh to
you" (James 4:8). He is always there within the
potential spiritual reach of all of us.

(2) Some are more emotional than others. Such people
weep openly at funerals and other such occasions
because their emotional systems demand such
outlets while others shed no tears; but the latter can

be touched just as deeply as the former. To label a
very emotional person as being more spiritual is
erroneous. To be spiritual, one does not have to
ascend on clouds during every worship service;
neither does he have to feel chills run up and down
his spine. To say "I didn't feel like worshipping
today" is admitting that we worship our feelings
rather than God.

(3) Every person's life is composed of mountains and
valleys. Most of our time is spent in the valleys,
plodding through the sands of daily existence.
But our God is a God of both the hills and the
valleys (1 Kings 20:26-29). He is with us just as much
in the valleys of routine living as He is there on the
mountains of our troubles and peaks of happiness.
Moses had his mountains: Horeb or Sinai, where he
witnessed the spectacle of the burning bush and later
received the Ten Commandments; Pisgah and its
peak called Nebo, from which he viewed the promised
land. This faithful leader of God's people spent most
of his 120 years, however, down in the valleys of
Egypt, Midian, and the sands of the wilderness
wanderings. God was there in both the mountains
and the valleys. Like Moses, our mountains draw us
away from the crowds and humdrum daily living to be
nearer to God.

(4) Strength is built little by little. Anyone who has
ever tried to tear a telephone book in half has
found it to be a very difficult, if not impossible,
task. Yet that book is composed of thin layer upon
layer. When those layers are bound one upon the
other, they constitute a bulwark of strength. In
the same sense a Christian's life is built layer upon
layer, and his strength comes from the accumulation
of seemingly uneventful acts, study, and services as
he obeys the will of God.

Perhaps a better understanding can be reached by
using a simple comparison. A tree grows by utilizing
the carbon dioxide found in the air, water from the
soil, and sunlight for energy. This process may go on
for years, without any seemingly spectacular events.

That unsightly log that we eventually put in our fireplace may not seem very glamorous, but it has slowly been storing energy from the sun throughout its existence. When fire is placed near the bark, the stored energy from the sun illuminates the entire room.

Christians are much like logs. For years and years our lives may seem uneventful, but we're slowly storing spiritual energy. "For precept must be upon precept . . . line upon line . . . here a little, and there a little" (Isaiah 28:10). When we are faithful in the study of the Word, perform our duties, and have the right attitude, we are storing divine power in our spiritual beings. As long as we remain in our self-sufficient, hard, outer covering we can never know how much potential energy and strength we possess; quite often we must get to the end of our ropes and cast ourselves upon God. It is the heat of the flame that releases the energy. Whether our lives will produce a bonfire or a feeble flicker when a match is struck to them depends primarily upon what is stored inside.

I don't think my life has been too different from those of most Christians. As I think back through the years, I can remember many mountains, or high points of my life, when I felt so close to God that it seemed as if I could reach out and touch Him: devotionals at camp while still a child; the happiness of holding each of my babies in my arms for the first time and thanking God for this new life formed as a fruit of our married love; the joy that comes from seeing someone whom you've taught walk down the aisle to be baptized; devotionals around a campfire with teenagers during mission meetings when the words of "O Lord My God" seemed to ascend to the heavens; the weeks of walking through the shadow of death and the comforting realization that I was not traveling alone; the first time, months later, when I attended church services propped in a lounge chair in the back of the building and shed tears because I was so thankful to be alive and back with God's people; one time when I was not hurting and I buried my face in my hands and wept a prayer of thanksgiving to God for something which I had taken for granted for so many previous years. Like any other child of God, the Lord has been with me through my mountains, but He was there when I needed Him because He also was with me through the uneventful valleys of my life when the foundations were being laid.

Suggestions for Class Use
Lesson Eight

1. Compare the problem of indifference with the problems which we usually consider as tribulations.
2. Discuss these Scriptures to prove that a Christian must actively seek his salvation all his life and remain faithful to the end: Revelation 2:10; John 15:1-7; 1 Corinthians 15:58.
3. What are the three groups of Christians considered in the lesson? (You may like to divide into three groups to discuss these different categories or you may prefer to follow the questions below.)
4. Why do some people never seem to change after baptism?
5. In the parable of the soils in Matthew 13 what happened to the seed that fell into stony places? Why?
6. What happens to a house when it is neglected (See Ecclesiastes 10:18).
7. What is the only hope for people in this category? What can you do to help them?
8. Some go through the outward forms of worship and yet have cynical hearts as cold as stone. What was the attitude of the priests in Malachi 1:13?
9. Amos denounced those who were "at ease in Zion." Describe their activities. (See Amos 6:1-6).
10. Discuss Christ's scathing denunciation of the scribes and Pharisees in Matthew 23:23-36.
11. The Christians at Ephesus had left their first love. What were they told to do? (See Revelation 2:4,5.)

12. What was the condition of the church at Laodicea? (See Revelation 3:15-22.)

13. In 2 Peter 1 what did the writer tell the Christians to do to make their calling and election sure?

14. What can happen to the things which we have heard? (See Hebrews 2:1.)

15. Discuss the traits of the older brother in Luke 15 that constitute negative goodness. What **were** his good points?

16. Compare the spiritual death of a Christian to the killing of the grass mentioned in the lesson.

17. Some worry because they "did not get anything out of the services." Are we supposed to "get something out" or "put something in"? What is the true meaning of worship?

18. Does a display of emotionalism indicate true spirituality? State your reasons.

19. Use an actual telephone book to illustrate the importance of one layer upon another in building the foundation of a Christian life. (Also use Isaiah 28:10.)

20. Compare the source of our spiritual energy with that which is stored in a tree. What releases the energy both in the tree and in a Christian's life?

21. Encourage the members of the class to discuss the mountains and valleys of their lives, stressing the importance of the seemingly uneventful foundations laid in our daily obedience to God.

9

The Cup of Unfaithful Children

 "Father, I've tried so hard to rear my child in an acceptable manner. He went to the services of the church regularly and attended all the Bible classes. I did my best to teach him while he was growing up, but now he is an unfaithful Christian. Where did I fail?"

Perhaps no other problem has weighed on the hearts of parents quite so heavily as that of wayward children. How right was Solomon when he said: "A foolish son is a grief to his father, and bitterness to her that bare him" (Proverbs 17:25). Previously in the same chapter the writer observed: "He that begetteth a fool doeth it to his sorrow: and the father of a fool hath no joy" (verse 21).

Today's children are not the only ones who have ever been rebellious. When 42 children mocked Elisha saying, "Go up, thou bald head" (2 Kings 2:23), two she bears promptly came out of the wood to attack them! In the Fifth Century B.C. Socrates wrote: "Our youth now love luxury. They have bad manners, contempt for authority; and they show disrespect for their elders, and love to chatter in places of exercise. They no longer rise when others enter the room. They contradict their parents; they chatter before company; they gobble their food and terrorize their teachers." (That was written in the Fifth Century?)

The Role of Parents

Few would deny that the parents have more influence in shaping the lives of their children than any other two people. "As the twig is bent so the tree is inclined."

The Scriptures abound with instructions for rearing children. God had faith that Abraham would command his descendants to keep the way of the Lord (Genesis 18:19). Exodus 13:8-16 instructs the Israelites to explain the significance of the Passover to their children. Explicit details for teaching are given in the following passages: Deuteronomy 4:9,10; Deuteronomy 6:6-9; Deuteronomy 11:18-21; Deuteronomy 31:12,13. David admonished his people to teach the law to their children "That the generation to come might know them . . . that they might set their hope in God, and not forget the works of God, but keep his commandments; and might not be as their fathers, a stubborn and rebellious generation" (Psalms 78:6-8). Isaiah was the writer of the familiar instructions for teaching others: "For precept must be upon precept . . . line upon line . . . here a little, and there a little" (Isaiah 28:10).

Discipline is strongly urged in the Old Testament. Spankings (with a rod!) are most emphatically taught in these passages from Proverbs: 13:24; 19:18; 22:15; 23:13,14; 29:15. Those who struck their parents, cursed them, and were stubborn and rebellious (even after chastening) were **stoned** to death (Exodus 21:15; Leviticus 20:9 and Deuteronomy 21:18-21).

The New Testament continues the same line of thought. "For God commanded, saying, Honour thy father and mother: and, He that curseth father or mother, let him die the death" (Matthew 15:4). "And, ye fathers, provoke not your children to wrath: but bring them up in the nurture and admonition of the Lord" (Ephesians 6:4). "Fathers, provoke not your children to anger, lest they be discouraged" (Colossians 3:21). Timothy's usefulness in the Lord's kingdom may be traced to the teaching which he received from his mother and grandmother (2 Timothy 1:5 and 3:15).

The end result of discipline, administered consistently and in the right manner (so the children won't be provoked to wrath—Ephesians 6:4 and Colossians 3:21), is the molding of children into disciples, or followers. When children come into this world, they are little barbarians who take what they want by hook or crook. They are to be led in the right direction by the setting of proper boundaries, or

standards of performance, so they can gain enough control
over themselves to develop their best qualities. Even
though youngsters will rebel from time to time against
these rules and will try to see how far they can go with their
parents, they find security in the knowledge that their
parents love them enough to care how they behave. A
parent who permits a child to have his own way by whining,
showing-off, and having tantrums is asking for trouble
later. Allowing a child to make everyone miserable **now** is
not going to make him more lovable when he is an **adult**.
Someone aptly observed that building boys is better than
mending men. Another unknown writer expressed a
parent's responsibility so well when he said: "What we put
into the thought stream of our children will appear in the
life stream of tomorrow."

Why Do They Leave?

Sometimes children from supposedly Christian homes
have nothing but contempt for the church. For centuries
parents have asked themselves for reasons. After studying
this problem in class and compiling information from a
number of parents who have faced this crisis, the following
factors seem to emerge.

(1) **Parents are often hypocrites.** They may take a very
active role in the affairs of the church, but their hearts are
not in the work. In the home children can clearly see a
discrepancy between what their mothers and daddies **say**
and what they actually **do**. Until a child is mature enough to
have his faith founded on the unshakable Word of God, his
primary life-line to things of a divine nature comes through
his mother and daddy. When the line is corroded, it is only
natural that the young one's faith will suffer. In this case,
the prodigal ones are the parents.

(2) **Divided homes impair development.** Rearing a child
in the right way has its share of problems when both
parents are faithful Christians, but the burdens multiply
when one has to shoulder the responsibility alone.
Sometimes the home is actually split by divorce. Others are
held together on the surface but are broken from within.
Such insecurity is bound to have its effect on the children.

In other marriages there is a reasonable amount of domestic tranquility, but one parent is pulling one way religiously while the other is tugging in the opposite direction or else is totally different. I have seen so many mothers and a few fathers who have put forth every reasonable effort to lead their children in the right manner, but they just couldn't accomplish the task alone.

(3) Some parents have expressed regret that they **discouraged** their children from obeying the Gospel because they seemed too young. Later, when these same parents urged their offspring to take the proper action, there was no interest.

(4) Some young people are very faithful as long as they remain at home; but **they become wayward when they leave the protective guidance of the home**, especially when they are bombarded with so many conflicting theories and actions in some **institutions of higher learning**. Others are drawn away through the influence of **unbelieving husbands or wives**. I have a number of statistics compiled by different ones in the brotherhood, all pointing to an undeniable fact: when one marries outside the church, the odds are against his remaining faithful to the Lord's cause. The influence of a lifetime partner exerts a tremendous pressure.

An Individual Responsibility

Although many factors may have an **influence** on a young person's development, ultimately the final **responsibility** rests upon his own shoulders. "But every one shall die for his own iniquity" (Jeremiah 31:30). Many good, hard-working, sincere Christians have read Proverbs 22:6 ("Train up a child in the way he should go: and when he is old, he will not depart from it"), and then blamed themselves for a wayward child. Scriptures must be understood in the light of what other passages teach. The admonition in Proverbs 22:6 is not a rule that works in every case; instead, it is a general principle. Consider the matter from a logical standpoint. If the eternal destiny of a young person is determined solely by the manner in which he is reared, then his damnation would be the fault of his parents; and the child would bear no blame. Such teaching completely disregards the fact that each person must stand upon his own feet at the judgment scene, regardless of what his hindrances may be, and give an account of **his** deeds (Romans 2:6). If each lost child could blame his parents, then each parent could blame **his** own parents and so on down the line until only Adam and Eve would be held responsible for the sins of all mankind. In my files I have a copy of an item entitled "Passing the Buck."

College Professor: "Such rawness in a student is a shame; poor high school preparation is to blame."

High School Principal: "It's plain to see the boy's a perfect fool! The fault lies strictly with the grammar school."

Grammar School Teacher: "I would that from such dolts I might be spared; they send them up to me so unprepared.!"

Kindergarten Teacher: "Ne'er such a lack of training did I see! What sort of person can that mother be?"

Mother: "You stupid child! But then, you're not to blame; your father's folks I know are all the same!"

While parents have a definite effect upon their children's destinies, **there are many other factors in each person's life.** Mothers and fathers cannot place an imaginary plastic bubble over their children to shield them from **all** evil influences. Many hours are spent away from home each day at school in the presence of both good and bad companions and teachers. As those who are so near and dear to us are gradually pushed out of the nest and taught the independence that is so vital for functioning properly in the adult world, it is only inevitable that they will feel the pull of the world. Proper training must be done early while minds are still pliable, because there will soon be a time of testing when parents must stand aside and prayerfully wait while their children try these teachings for themselves. The parable of the prodigal son in Luke 15 is an example of this principle.

A child's basic temperament is also greatly influenced by his heredity, which includes many factors. Every parent should realize that his offspring is not a carbon copy of himself, nor can that child be manipulated like a robot. No two children in a family are alike. Neither are they reared exactly in the same manner because the mother and father respond differently to each child. They are given to us like tuned instruments upon which we try to play the proper melody, but it's difficult to make a fiddle sound like a harp.

The Scriptures give example after example of outstanding children of God who produced evil offspring. Eli had the primary responsibility for the teaching of Samuel, who was such a faithful leader; yet Eli's own sons (Hophni and Phinehas) made themselves vile and he restrained them not (1 Samuel 3:13). Even Samuel's sons failed to walk in the ways of their father; consequently, the people wanted a king to rule over them (1 Samuel 8:1-5). Isaac's twin boys, Jacob and Esau, reacted differently to essentially the same training. Out of Jacob's twelve sons, only one truly remained faithful to God throughout his life. David was a man after God's own heart (1 Samuel 13:14), and yet he fathered the rebellious Absalom. Before David's death he charged his son Solomon to walk in the ways of God that he might prosper and continue to have an heir upon the throne (1 Kings 2:1-4). The wise king who said: "Train up a child in the way he should go. . ." fathered Rehoboam, who was nothing but trouble for the kingdom. If the wisest man who ever lived had this kind of trouble with his son, think about the rest of us! Even the earthly parents of Christ did not train all their children to be believers (See John 7:5; Matthew 13:57; Mark 6:3,4.).

Conclusion

While parents are commanded to train their children properly and will be condemned for failure to do so, there are other factors which also influence a child's thinking. The ultimate decision for right or wrong is left up to the individual and the responsibility is his, just as the prodigal son accepted the blame for his actions when he said, "I have sinned" (Luke 15:21). A faithful parent who has done all within his power to train his child properly and then sorrows as he becomes unfaithful must continue to pray, keep the lines of communication open, put in an appropriate word when possible, and wait to see whether or not the seed fell into an honest heart. (Remember that it was the **same** seed, or teaching, that was sown in the different hearts in the parable of the soils.) There is always hope that the wayward child will "remember the word of the Lord" as did Peter, and weep (Luke 22:61,62).

If a parent has properly taught his unfaithful child, that parent can expect the same mercy that God has promised to any Christian who converts another person who is eventually lost (1 Corinthians 3:10-15).

Suggestions for Class Use
Lesson Nine

1. Is youthful rebellion a new problem? Discuss Elisha's problem in 2 Kings 2:23,24 and also the remarks made by Socrates.
2. "Almost every normal teenager alternately loves and hates his parents." Do you agree or disagree?
3. Assign one class member the task of explaining the Jewish system of instruction for its young. Use the verses mentioned in the lesson in addition to outside references. How does our instruction compare?
4. The New Testament continues the same line of thought concerning the necessity of disciplining, or training, the young. Why is it incorrect to think of discipline only as correction or punishment for wrongdoing? How can faulty discipline provoke children to anger? (See Ephesians 6:4 and Colossians 3:21.)
5. Ask each class member to explain his own practical theory of discipline in a few sentences (ideas which have proven to be useful).
6. Sometimes children become unfaithful because their parents are hypocrites. Discuss the importance of **living** what we teach. Is there any such thing as a perfect parent? Is it damaging for him to admit his errors to his children and ask for their forgiveness and help?
7. How can a home divided by divorce, different religious beliefs, or bickering cause resentment and confusion in children?
8. Some children never obey the Gospel because they

were discouraged when they were young. Discuss the best course of action to take when a very young child expresses such a desire.

9. Others leave the faith when they leave home for college or for marriage to an unbeliever. What can be done to prevent this?

10. Although many factors influence a child's development, the final responsibility rests upon whose shoulders?

11. Discuss Jeremiah 31:29,30 using a comparison with the Ezekiel 18.

12. Discuss Proverbs 22:6 (preferably in smaller groups at first). If a child becomes wayward, is it always because the parents did not properly teach him by word and example? State your reasons.

13. Parents are not the only ones who influence the thinking of young people. Who are some of the others? How much control do you feel that a parent should have over his child's associates?

14. We may say that we rear all our children alike, but is this actually the case? Why?

15. The Scriptures cite many cases of outstanding Bible characters whose children were evil. What were some of the sins of Eli's sons? (See 1 Samuel 2:12-17 and 3:11-14.) What was wrong with Samuel's sons? (See 1 Samuel 8:1-5.)

16. Discuss the troubles which Isaac, Jacob, David, Solomon, and the parents of Christ had with some of their children.

17. Discuss the parable of the prodigal son in Luke 15. Was the father in error in allowing the younger son to leave? Actually there were two prodigal sons. What were the sins of the older son?

18. When a Christian parent has faithfully taught his child by both word and deed only to see him leave the faith, what is his best course of action then? (The class might like to talk with the members who have been successful in handling such a problem and then report to the group.)

19. How does the principle taught in 1 Corinthians 3:10-15 apply to Christian parents?

10

The Cup of Loneliness

"Father, my days seem so long and lonely. The telephone seldom rings. Most of my friends have forgotten me. No one really cares whether I live or die. Day after day I sit here, just wishing that someone, **anyone**, would show a little interest in me."

Loneliness is a universal problem that has plagued mankind since the beginning of history. When God formed Adam, He said: "It is not good that the man should be alone" (Genesis 2:18), and Eve's creation was the answer to that problem. Adam's son, Cain, must have felt a sense of loneliness when he was cursed with a life as a fugitive and a vagabond for the killing of Abel, his brother, because the murderer cried out, "My punishment is greater than I can bear" (Genesis 4:13). The mind of Moses was shaped in the crucible of the lonely desert plains of Midian. It was David, hunted as a partridge by King Saul in the wilderness area, who said: "No man cared for my soul" (Psalms 142:4) and also: "I am forgotten as a dead man out of mind" (Psalms 31:12). Elijah fled from the wrath of Jezebel into the wilderness of Beersheba and there sat down under a juniper tree, totally dejected and wishing that he might die (1 Kings 19:1-4). Christ, our Supreme Example, must have also experienced loneliness on several occasions in His life: His temptation in the wilderness (Luke 4:1-13), the desertion of His followers and kin (John 6:66 and 7:5), the fleeing of the disciples in the garden (Matthew 26:56), the hurt of Peter's denial (Luke 22:54-62). There was also the time when He was suspended on the cross with the sins of mankind on His shoulders, and He cried out in agony: "My

God, my God, why hast thou forsaken me?" (Matthew 27:46). Paul, who spent much time in desolate prison cells, experienced this same feeling when he said: "No man stood with me, but all men forsook me" (2 Timothy 4:16).

Today loneliness is cited as the primary problem of 80 percent of those who seek psychiatric help. It is also a major cause of suicides and alcoholism. The basic human need for contact with others, which is just as necessary as food and water for survival, is not confined to one age group. Children, teenagers, young parents, older parents whose children have left home, and the aged all share alike in this malady.

Definition of Loneliness

When I was teaching this subject in a class, I asked the members to tell me what connotations came into their minds when I mentioned the word **loneliness.** I received such responses as: **no one to talk to, tears, lack of something to do, no one to do for, not being needed, physically unable** and others. Loneliness means different things to different people.

Loneliness is being a new child in school where everyone else already has friends. Loneliness is being the only teenager (even among fellow Christians) who takes a stand for the Truth by refusing to participate in questionable activities. Loneliness is not making the team or winning the election. Loneliness is those first months away from home at college. Loneliness is being a new mother who is confined to her home most of the winter with a sick child. Loneliness is moving into a different town. Loneliness is the emptiness a parent feels when the last child leaves home. Loneliness is lying in a hospital bed for so long that the walls seem to close in. Loneliness is sitting by the window of a nursing home on a rainy afternoon, wishing that someone, anyone, would come by. Loneliness is returning to an empty house after the funeral of a loved one. Loneliness is the realization that you can never go back home again.

There is a vast difference in being alone and being lonely, although the former **can** be a factor contributing to the cause of loneliness. Just as we all need human companionship, so do we need periods of aloneness for both our mental and physical well-being. Most of the great contributions made in civilization have been conceived and nourished in solitude. The psalmist recognized this truth when he penned: "He leadeth me beside the still waters. He restoreth my soul" (Psalms 23:2,3). Our Lord knew the healing qualities of solitude when He left the crowds and sought times of quietness. A person may spend time alone and yet never be lonely if he has good self-esteem. He is never alone if he is a friend to himself.

There is also a vast difference in the **natural loneliness** that is the common lot of all mankind at one time or another and the **loneliness that is a crippling sickness** that alienates one from all that is beautiful and worthwhile in this life. If we are completely truthful, each one of us will have to admit that he has experienced the pangs of loneliness during his life as the result of being a human in trying situations. The primary difference between this loneliness and the devastating kind is a matter of intensity and duration. The normal person recognizes loneliness as a temporary condition and takes corrective measures. The neurotic individual takes such great delight in wallowing in the self-pity of his loneliness that he gradually loses his ability to pull himself out of the mire. His loneliness gnaws at his mind until it becomes an obsession.

Causes

Anyone who has studied educational psychology and has taught in the classroom is aware of the truth that his greatest problem is usually not the aggressive little imp who is constantly getting into trouble but the quiet, withdrawn student who has no friends. Studies have been made of presidential assassins and would-be assassins. They are the outcasts, the people who are alienated, frustrated, and forgotten. They are the ones who desire recognition so desperately that they are willing to go to drastic measures to achieve it. Such people are constantly sending out seldom noticed signals for help; they are saying, "Please understand me." A number of factors contribute to this kind of excessive loneliness.

(1) A person's **basic temperament**, which is genetically determined, greatly influences his outlook on life. In 400 B.C. Hippocrates classified man's temperaments into these four categories: phlegmatic (low, lethargic), choleric (quick, fiery, passionate), sanguine (warm, cheerful, enthusiastic, optimistic), and melancholic (somber, grave, sad). While a person's emotional outlook may be influenced greatly by his genes, it can be modified if he sincerely wants to do so.

(2) The **population explosion** has had a detrimental effect upon the closeness of mankind. People used to live in isolated communities where they cared about the joys and sorrows of one another. Today's urban society is crowded with people—all going their separate, busy ways with little regard or concern for their fellow-creatures. Crowds can be so lonely.

(3) Paradoxically, **self-love** is an underlying cause of loneliness. A person completely wrapped up in himself is not going to be appealing to others and will naturally be overlooked. The people who complain that no one spoke to them at a church service are usually the ones who don't put forth the effort to make any friends. They never speak first or even try to smile at the person sitting next to them. Such individuals are so conscious of **their** feelings and are so afraid **they** will be hurt that they crawl into their shells instead of venturing outside themselves to make others happy. It was Joseph Newton who said, "People are lonely because they build walls instead of bridges." They blame everyone but themselves.

(4) Lonely people have **no sense of direction, no compelling goals in life**. Drifting aimlessly gives a person ample time to notice and harbor even an unintentional slight by someone. One who is engrossed in a cause and a purpose greater than himself has no time to notice how others may treat him. He is too big to hold grudges.

The Solution

Human beings **will** react to loneliness in one way or another. So often the reactions are negative, destructive ones: worry, overeating, depression, drugs, alcohol, sleeping too much or else insomnia, promiscuity, psycho-somatic illnesses, and others.

First of all, one should realize that occasional loneliness and feeling low is only a normal part of the cycle of life. It is entirely **abnormal** for each day to be the same. There is a Chinese proverb that says, "There is a time for fishing and a time for drying one's nets." Solomon expressed the same idea a little differently when he wrote: "To every thing there is a season, and a time to every purpose under the heaven . . . a time to weep, and a time to laugh. . ." (Ecclesiastes 3:1-8).

An occasional blue day can be brightened with the realization that "this too shall pass." We do not have to constantly **dwell** in the cellars of our emotions. While waiting for nature to take its healing course, we can help speed matters along by **acting** cheerful and optimistic whether we feel that way or not. William James, the noted psychologist, stated: "Action seems to follow feeling, but really action and feeling go together; and by regulating the action, which is under the more direct control of the will, we can indirectly regulate the feeling, which is not . . . Thus, the sovereign voluntary path to cheerfulness, if your cheerfulness is lost, is to sit up cheerfully and to act and speak as if cheerfulness were already there." It was Abraham Lincoln who said: "Most folks are about as happy as they make up their minds to be."

The person who suffers from the more serious, neurotic type of loneliness must first of all admit that the only real solution lies within himself. Since little, if anything, can be done to change his heredity or the crowded conditions of the world (discussed in the previous section), he will have to focus his attention upon the last two factors: self-love and no real sense of direction in life.

Self-love can be overcome by thinking of others. Everyone should have a healthy respect for himself, but there is a vast difference between self-respect and a selfish love for self to the exclusion of others. Psychiatrist Alfred Adler gave a remedy for loneliness when he said, "Try to think every day how you can please someone." Such action causes us to stop thinking of ourselves, a major cause of fear and worry. It is virtually impossible to be lonely when

we are engrossed in seeking ways to make life more
pleasant for others. Thoughtfulness need not require
money. The gift of our time is perhaps the most priceless
present we can give. Epictetus, the Greek philosopher,
wisely said, "What I made I lost; what I gave I had." Christ
knew the best way to overcome loneliness and lead a happy
life when He advised: "He that loseth his life for my sake
shall find it" (Matthew 10:39) and also, "It is more blessed
to give than to receive" (Acts 20:35). In Luke 6:38 He said:
"Give, and it shall be given unto you; good measure,
pressed down, and shaken together, and running over, shall
men give into your bosom. **For with the same measure that
ye mete withal it shall be measured to you again.**" The
people with the most friends are the ones who have gone
out of their way to be thoughtful to others. Instead of
pouting or wallowing in self-pity because nobody ever pays
any attention to us, we should have enough gumption to get
out and find someone whose day needs brightening by some
small act of kindness. Even those who are physically unable
to venture outside their homes can bring countless joy to
others through the mail or by telephone. As we change **our**
outlook toward others by viewing them as people we can
help, we will find that **their** actions toward us will also
change.

A lack of direction in life must be changed consciously.
"An aim in life is the only fortune worth finding" (Robert
Louis Stevenson). Life is out of focus for so many people
who seem to be treading water and getting nowhere at all.
The life of such a person is just about as futile as that of one
that fights by beating the air (1 Corinthians 9:26). Such
people have never taken the time to find themselves, to
evaluate their lives to know what they really want, what
their abilities are, and what brings the most satisfaction to
them. It requires a great deal of effort and discipline to set a
goal in life and then stick with it; many never even bother
to try. Just as a river is crooked because it follows the
course of least resistance, so are people's lives warped
when they have no goals or ambitions. "Apathy can only be
overcome by enthusiasm, and enthusiasm can only be
aroused by an ideal which takes the imagination by storm"
(Arnold Toynbee).

Great achievements are not the result of luck or chance. Others may not be aware of the dreams, the hard work, and the disappointments involved; but all of these are factors in success. The following suggestions will help a person set and attain such an ideal.

(1) **Pinpoint what you want.** Don't dissipate. Concentrate! Make your goal clear and specific. Paul said: "This **one** thing I do" (Philippians 3:13). While goals must be reasonably attainable, aim high. The greatest tragedy is not failure but aiming too low. It was Robert Browning who said that a man's reach should exceed his grasp. After we have built our castles in the air, we then have to get busy and put foundations under them by breaking the achievement of that aim into steps. Our ultimate aim in life may be so high that it seems discouraging even to try, but we **can** take one step at a time. Smaller victories give us the satisfaction and incentive to keep on trying. The rungs of a ladder were never meant to rest upon but to serve as a place for one's foot until he could reach the next one. As we achieve with each step, we find that we can do even more tomorrow. The mind is elastic. The more we try to do, the more we find we **can** do. Humans tend to gravitate toward that which they love and glorify. Whatever is inside will shape the outside. The good, pure life will attract people with similar ideals.

We've spoken in generalities about aims or goals in life. Now let's be specific. Aims involving wealth, prominence, or social position will be left behind when each of us dies. The only thing that will endure forever must be of a spiritual nature. Christ means nothing until He means everything. As Christians, we should get a clear mental picture of the person we hope to become and then set out to attain that goal by logical, sequential steps. It's not enough merely to say that we want to become better Bible students. What do we hope to accomplish by next month in our study? By the end of the year? Five years from now? How many sick people do we plan to visit this week? This month? Have we selected one person whom we hope to convert this year? How many do we plan to win next year? Remember, in the harvest we reap what we sow in the springtime.

(2) **Earnestly desire your goal.** As lofty as our aims may
be and regardless of how well we've broken them down into
steps, it will all be useless until we have kindled enough
ambition to put forth the necessary effort. The result will
be in proportion to the intensity of our desires and can only
come from within. The incentive for that yearning can come
from a number of different factors. Discontent with present
conditions pulls some people down; in others it prods them
on to better things. Some want to change if they have been
deeply hurt or have felt that something has been missing in
their lives. Many have been inspired to continue trying by
vividly imagining themselves as achieving that goal. Others
have to be challenged. How well I remember what the
doctor told me concerning the restoration of a damaged
hand: "What you eventually will be able to do with that
hand will depend upon how much you **want** the use of it and
how **hard** you are willing to work with it." The effort
required two different braces and several months of painful
exercising, but I met his challenge!

(3) **Be willing to pay the price.** No one (except a thief)
would think of walking out of a jewelry store with a
diamond ring unless he has first paid the price for it.
Diamonds are not free; we have to give something in
exchange for them. As lofty as goals may be and regardless
of how much we desire them, they will never be reached
unless we are willing to give up something in order to
achieve them. They require not only aspiration and
inspiration but also perspiration. "Whatsoever ye do, do it
heartily" (Colossians 3:23). Occasionally an opportunity will
knock at our door, but most of the time we have to get out
in the bushes and search. "The people who get on in this
world are the people who look for the circumstances they
want, and if they can't find them, make them" (George
Bernard Shaw).

Once we have decided the direction of our lives and have
broken the acquisition of the goal into logical steps, it
requires a great deal of perseverance to train ourselves to
stay on that chosen course and not deviate from it. Just as
bad habits are made by the repetition of undesirable deeds,
so are good habits made by consciously repeating desirable
acts. In order to establish a habit it is best to declare our

intentions publically and not allow an exception to occur until the action becomes automatic. Horace Mann said, "Habit is a cable; we weave a thread of it every day, and at last we cannot break it."

William James, the famous psychologist, taught: "The man who has daily inured himself to habits of concentrated attention, energetic volition and self-denial will stand like a tower when everything rocks about him and when his softer fellow mortals are winnowed like chaff in the blast. Sow an action and you reap a habit; sow a habit and you reap a character; sow a character and you reap a destiny."

Conclusion

Everyone faces loneliness at one time or another. Its seriousness depends upon its intensity and its duration. The best remedies are learning to reach out to others and the developing of a direction or aim in life that is so consuming that we have no time to be lonely.

Suggestions for Class Use
Lesson Ten

1. Trace the thread of loneliness that runs throughout the Scriptures by noting the lives of Adam, Cain, Moses, David, Elijah, Christ, and Paul.
2. Why does loneliness affect so many different age groups?
3. Ask each class member to write his definition of loneliness on a slip of paper. Collect these and read aloud to the class.
4. What is the difference between being alone and being lonely?
5. What is the difference between the loneliness which everyone experiences at one time or another and the loneliness that is a sickness?
6. Before class time select a panel of four people to discuss the primary causes of loneliness. Encourage them to add their own ideas.
7. What are some negative reactions to loneliness?

8. Can acting cheerful help one out of a temporary slump? Do you agree with William James' philosophy concerning feeling and action? State your reasons.

9. Loneliness can be lessened when we lose ourselves in service to others. Read and discuss Matthew 10:39, Acts 20:35, and Luke 6:38 in relation to this thought.

10. Giving to others need not require money. Discuss examples of the giving of our time. Be specific.

11. People who are sincerely warm and outgoing are seldom lonely. Think of the people whose company you most enjoy. What traits make their companionship attractive?

12. How can an older person, confined in his activities and abilities to reach out to others, cope with loneliness?

13. Some are lonely because they have no direction in life. Help the class members set some definite goals by answering the following questions. (These questions will have some merit if they are simply discussed in class, but lasting benefits will result only if they are answered in writing by each member.)

I. Who am I? (Plato said that the unexamined life is not worth living.)

   A. Strengths
      1. What are my favorite pastimes?
      2. What are my special abilities?
      3. What brings me the greatest sense of satisfaction?
      4. For what do I receive the most compliments?
      5. Others

   B. Weaknesses
      1. What hurts me most?
      2. What are my main fears?
      3. What embarrasses me most?
      4. What do I shun or avoid?
      5. Others

II. Where am I going?
    A. Personal relationship with God
       1. Study areas
       2. Prayer life
       3. Other

This Week	One Year	Five Years

    B. Christian graces
       (love, joy, peace, patience, gentleness, goodness,
       faith, meekness, temperance)

This Week	One Year	Five Years

    C. Family
       1. Husband
       2. Children
       3. Others

This Week	One Year	Five Years

    D. Outreach to others
       1. Their spiritual and emotional needs
          a. Bible teacher (How do I plan to improve
             myself?)
          b. Converting the lost
          c. Strengthening the weak
       2. Their physical needs
          a. Poverty
          b. Sickness

This Week	One Year	Five Years

III. How will I get there? (One day at a time)
    A. Near the end of each day make a tentative list of
       the things you hope to accomplish tomorrow.
    B. Rate each one in the order of its importance.

C. Tomorrow stay with number one until it is completed. Then go to number two and so on. Don't worry if you can't finish the list. You have done what is most important.

D. At the close of each day, review what you have done. Ask forgiveness for the wrongs and then forget them. Offer the day back to God as your gift to Him.

E. Keep a record of your daily lists. Every month look them over and evaluate what you're doing with your goals in life. Are you accomplishing what you really want to do?

"I am not what I ought to be. I am not what I wish to be, and I am not what I hope to be, but by the grace of God I am not what I once was" (John Newton).

11

The Cup of Sickness

 "Father, I have tried to serve Thee and be faithful. Why did this illness have to strike right at the time when my family needs me most and so many things ought to be done? The cost is staggering. What have I done to have this burden placed upon my shoulders?"

Cries of anguish precipitated by sickness are not new to modern mankind; they have been heard since the dawn of time. It is possible that Adam or Eve lost a beloved mate to the ravages of some sort of disease. The Egyptians suffered an excruciating illness when the plague of boils was sent upon them (Exodus 9:8-12). The Jewish nation was given strict laws concerning the proper care of its sick. (Leviticus 13 and 14 deal with the regulations concerning lepers.) King David dealt kindly with Jonathan's lame son, Mephibosheth, whose inability to walk resulted from no fault of his own. The Shunammite woman must have felt the same despair as modern mothers when her son was stricken with a serious illness. Hezekiah was so sick that he turned his face to the wall in prayer (2 Kings 20:1-11). Christ proved His divinity by healing sick people. The cases of illness in the New Testament are so numerous that there will be no time for elaboration upon them in this lesson. (Even Paul said that he preached the gospel through infirmity of the flesh in Galatians 4:13).Illness has plagued mankind since the beginning of time and will continue to do so until the world comes to an end.

Why?

Sometimes people become quite angry with God when sickness strikes. Perhaps they feel that the badge of Christianity should give them automatic immunity to disease. Christians will face the same problems as any other human being, **but they can face them in a different manner.**

If we're going to blame anyone, it should be Adam and Eve instead of God. At the beginning of time these two were given the freedom of choice. Their decision carried with it the natural consequence of eventual death, and the results will follow mankind as long as he is here on this earth. Barring the second coming of Christ, we know that one day death will be our lot. Actually the dying process begins around the age of 25 as the body begins its automatic deterioration. Various parts of the body begin to give us trouble until most of us finally succumb to some sort of sickness or tragic accident. It's really only a matter of time until one of these factors will take its toll.

In addition to the inevitable deterioration of the body, which originated with Adam and Eve, we also suffer illness because of another factor. Generally speaking, man is unhappy when he lives alone, isolated from other human beings. In the beginning God said that it was not good that man should be alone (Genesis 2:18). Enjoying the benefits of companionship with other people also carries with it a logical hazzard. The carelessness of others can inflict disease and also the heartbreak associated with accidents. God does not bring these infirmities upon us. People do. Even though we would be safer living a life of solitude, such existence is not worth the attached price tag.

In addition to the ravages of disease and the suffering brought about by the carelessness of others, let's not forget our own carelessness and neglect. If we are completely honest, each of us will have to admit that we do not always properly care for our bodies. Much of our sickness is caused by our own neglect.

Ordinary Illnesses

Since the last chapter of this book will deal with the

problem of terminal illnesses, the remainder of this study will focus upon the problems connected with the usual sickness which most people must endure at one time or another and also the problems connected with long-term or lifetime physical limitations.

Very rare indeed is the person who has not been confined to his bed at home or to a hospital room for a number of weeks due to necessary surgery, a broken limb, a communicable disease or some other misfortune. The following suggestions may help him bear his misfortune in a better manner.

(1) **Accept this temporary misfortune with the proper attitude.** Review the section which considered the reasons for sickness. When a person can accept such setbacks with the right attitudes, half the battle has already been won. Resentment or blaming the calamity upon God or anyone else only slows the healing process.

(2) **Recognize the fact that solitude has its own benefits.** All of us are too busy doing things which we feel simply cannot wait. Sometimes we need to be shown that those matters **can** wait and quite often someone else can do them just as well as we can. Any musician is aware of the fact that the rests in a musical score are just as important as the notes which are played. The same is true in our lives. When we consider the overall melody of life, we can clearly understand how beautiful the rests have been. Although permanent solitude can produce insanity, temporary solitude can be the breeding place for some very worthwhile ideas which somehow never seem to surface during the grind of daily existence. "Conversation enriches the understanding, but solitude is the school of genius" (Edward Gibbon). Thomas Carlyle expressed the same idea a little differently when he said: "Silence is the element in which great things fashion themselves." Eugene O'Neill, the famous playwright, drifted aimlessly until tuberculosis confined him to a sanatorium at the age of twenty-five. It was here that he found the leisure time to begin writing his plays. Many wise people have used the time of their confinement to begin or complete many worthwhile projects.

A break from the busyness of worldly cares gives time for introspection. How tragic it is when we live with a complete stranger, never really understanding ourselves. Illness gives us time to meditate upon our goals in life. A close call can make us sit up and take notice of what we really want out of life and what we are doing to reach those goals.

Illness induces humility as we realize that we are not self-sufficient. No matter how much influence we may exert in a worldly sense, disease strikes all. It is good for everyone to realize, at one time or another, the limitations of his power. The cleansing fire of suffering can purge a person of wrong attitudes and make him fit for worthwhile purposes. Milton aptly said: "Who best can suffer, best can do." His **Paradise Lost**, written after his blindness, is a concrete example of how stimulating suffering can be.

Sickness makes us all aware of precious little treasures which we were too busy to notice before. An unknown sage said, "For health and wealth to be enjoyed, they must be interrupted." The thoughtfulness of our families, the robin singing outside our window, the crackling of the burning logs in the fireplace - all assume a new significance when we have the time to stop and notice.

(3) **Illness teachs us how much thoughtfulness can mean.** Most of us mean well, but we're so busy that we carelessly overlook opportunities to do little things for those who are sick. Sometimes we have to be placed flat on our backs before we can truly understand how very much a card can mean, and how much we appreciate the concern others show to our families when we can't care for them ourselves. First-hand experience is a stern teacher, but her lessons are not easily forgotten. Our thoughts are automatically turned toward others as we seek ways to repay the kindnesses which were shown to us.

(4) **Sickness makes us more understanding of the tribulations of others.** It is a simple matter for a healthy person to criticize those who dwell in unhealthy bodies and freely give them advice. Quite often that advice turns sour on the tongue when we must eat our own words. We cannot possibly know how others feel and suffer unless we have walked in similar shoes.

As more exposed to suffering and distress;
Thence, also, more alive to tenderness.

William Wordsworth

(5) **Illness helps us count our blessings.** Most of us skip blithely through life, expecting good health as a natural right. Once we have been stricken with some form of serious physical malady, we tend to view healthy bodies, even reasonably healthy ones, in a new perspective.

One day while I was being fitted with orthopedic shoes, a woman sitting next to me was bitterly complaining about the necessity of wearing such shoes. Granted, they are not the most beautiful things in the world. At any other time I probably would have grumbled along with her, but I had just seen a doctor in a rehabilitation hospital. So many people there would never walk a step again. How thankful they would have been to wear **any** sort of shoe if only they **could** walk. I slip mine on each day with a sense of thankfulness that I **can walk** and that there is a shoe which can bring some relief.

Physical Handicaps

Most of us can muster enough courage for a reasonably short illness, even a serious one, but patience tends to wear thin when an infirmity drags on for years with no hope of relief. Constant pain saps our strengrth and also affects our outlook on life. Friends may be very attentive during a normal illness, but they fade in number as the days turn into weeks, the weeks lengthen into months, and months drag into years.

People with physical handicaps usually fall into one of two categories. Some bear their infirmities with great resentment and make the lives of all around them miserable also. Others seem to have a special grace and are able to rise above whatever their limitations might be to truly live a life of beauty instead of simply existing. The difference has to lie within.

The same principles discussed in chapters three and four are especially applicable to this problem.

As it was mentioned earlier, a person shouldn't learn to sail a boat in a storm. Neither can any of us adequately cope with physical handicaps or any other type of problem unless the **proper foundation** has been laid. Trust in God and the proper use of prayer are not learned in hot water. The godly acceptance of such tribulations is the result of many years of study and doing His will in good times. Also, **Christian friendships** should be developed throughout our lives, not just during the time of need.

Most of us would throw up our hands in despair if we knew today what troubles we would face in our lifetimes. They were never meant to be dealt with all at once. It is amazing what a load we can bear on our shoulders if we can learn to carry it **only one day at a time.** The same is true of a person who knows that he will never be any better. Such a thought is staggering. But he **can** shoulder it for **today.**

In addition to the general principles laid down earlier (proper foundation, Christian friendships, and learning to bear one day's burdens at a time), let's be more specific in suggestions for the physically handicapped.

(1) **Realize that everyone has handicaps.** While the ones that result in physical deformities are more apparent, everyone has limitations of some sort. Helen Keller felt that it was better to remain in physical darkness with full use of the other senses, feeling, and mind than to have good eyes that fail to notice so many worthwhile things in life. The **real** handicap is to have normal eyes and yet never pause long enough to absorb the beauty of a sunset or notice the magical wonder in the face of a child. Envy, selfishness, distrust, and other vices may not be as noticeable as crippled legs; but diseases of the attitude can also be crippling.

(2) **Check the impulse of self-pity.** Asking for the sympathy of others only intensifies the effect of the physical abnormality. To envy normal people impedes progress.

(3) **Turn your thoughts outward.** This principle, which is beneficial to practically any problem, is especially applicable to the physically handicapped person. The best way to get our minds off our own problems is to go out of the way to bring a little happiness into the lives of others.

When I was injured in the automobile accident, I received a most encouraging letter from a woman whom I had never met. For a number of years she has been confined to a wheel chair in a nursing home as the result of rheumatoid arthritis. Instead of dwelling upon her own misfortunes, she spends her days trying to bring cheer to others. For example, in a recent year she sent over nine hundred cards to brighten the days of those who were sick, in sorrow, or in need of some kind of encouragement. It would be so easy for her to fall back on the excuse that her hands are deformed and she can't write with ease. I would venture to say that her acts of thoughtfulness have kept her hands limber in addition to enlarging her heart of compassion.

(4) **Accept the challenge of developing yourself to the fullest in whatever state you find yourself.** Just as an artist shows his ability by restricting himself to expression by means of oils and canvas and a sculptor produces a masterpiece by chiseling a beautiful form from a hard piece of rock, so does the handicapped person display the skill of an artist when he is able to live a life of beauty in a restricted body.

Not too long ago I spoke to a group of teenage girls at a meeting planned especially for young people. In the hall I saw a severely deformed boy on crutches. I smiled casually in passing, and he responded with one of the sweetest smiles I have ever seen. It was the look of compassion and victory that could only result from the winning of an internal struggle. I did not see that same depth of feeling in the faces of the normal young people there. It made me stop and wonder who really had the handicap.

Some of the most soul-stirring poetry that I have ever read was penned by a woman who originally planned to be a concert pianist but was left hopelessly crippled by arthritis by the time she was twenty. It was necessary for her to use a writing board placed above the bed while lying flat on her back.

There is a vast difference between giving up and accepting conditions as they are. In the latter situation the person realizes that there are some things that are utterly impossible for him to do. Instead of becoming discouraged, such people develop themselves to the fullest within the

boundaries over which they have no control. After all, isn't
this the essence of the teaching in the parable of the talents
(Matthew 25:14-30)?

(5) **Realize that this handicap is only for a limited time
and things will be better one day.** Most of us can stand anything for a little while if we have the hope that conditions
will eventually improve. The faithful child of God has the
promise that one day there will be no more sickness, no
sorrow, no tears. Sickness and handicaps cause us to yearn
for something better. Such impediments serve as stimuli to
help us live better and strive for Heaven. They are actually
blessings in disguise.

I would like to close this chapter with a poem that has
meant a great deal to me, for it expresses so beautifully
some rather difficult lessons I learned the hard way. I have
tried to trace the authorship but could only find that it is
credited to an anonymous soldier of the Confederacy.

> I asked God for strength,
>   that I might achieve -
> I was made weak,
>   that I might learn humbly to obey.
>
> I asked for help,
>   that I might do greater things -
> I was given infirmity,
>   that I might do better things.
>
> I asked for riches,
>   that I might be happy -
> I was given poverty,
>   that I might be wise.
>
> I asked for all things,
>   that I might enjoy life -
> I was given life,
>   that I might enjoy all things.
>
> I got nothing that I asked for,
>   but everything I had hoped for,

Despite myself,
  my prayers were answered.
I am, among all men
  most richly blessed.

Suggestions for Class Use
Lesson Seven

1. Trace examples of sickness through the Scriptures, adding to the ones given in the lesson.
2. If Christians are going to face the same problems as everyone else, what is the advantage in being a Christian?
3. At what time did sickness and the dying process come into this world? If we are going to blame anyone, who should it be?
4. How can association with other human beings inflict sickness upon us?
5. How can our own carelessness contribute to our ill health?

(At this point the teacher may wish to divide the class into two groups to discuss the problems of ordinary illnesses and those connected with physical handicaps.The following questions can be used by the groups in their discussions or by the entire class in a general discussion.)

Ordinary Illnesses
6. What is the proper attitude toward any sort of sickness? Why is it wrong to blame the misfortune on God?
7. Discuss at least five benefits of the solitude which so often accompanies illness.
8. Elicit from the class members some practical lessons on the true meaning of thoughtfulness which they have learned from their own periods of confinement.
9 It is easy to offer advice, but can we really understand how others feel unless we have experienced a similar problem?
10. Why does illness make us more aware of our blessings?

Physical Handicaps

11. How can a physical handicap or any lengthly illness be a greater strain than an ordinary sickness, even a critical one?

12. What are the advantages of laying a proper foundation of faith, developing Christian friendships, and learning to carry only one day's burdens at a time **before** illness strikes?

13. Do you agree or disagree with the statement that everyone has handicaps? To what extent?

14. How does self-pity only retard progress?

15. How can our own problems be lessened by thinking of ways to help others bear their burdens? Does this seem paradoxical?

16. Be specific in suggesting ways that a handicapped person can develop himself to the fullest within his limitations. Relate to the parable of the talents (Matthew 25:14-30).

17. How can constant pain and frustrations here on this earth cause us to yearn for something better?

18. Discuss this statement: "A misfortune that causes one to draw closer to God is not a burden; it is a blessing in disguise."

12

The Cup of Death ~ A Loved One

"Father, it seems that I just cannot give up my loved one. He was so young and the future seemed so promising. Why was he taken from me?"

"Have the gates of death been opened unto thee? or hast thou seen the doors of the shadow of death?" (Job 38:17).

If death has not knocked at your door yet, it is just down the street; death is just as much a part of the cycle of life as birth. "To every thing there is a season, and a time of every purpose under the heaven: a time to be born, and a time to die" (Ecclesiastes 3:1,2). Numerous Scriptures warn us that life is short and fleeting at its very best. "It is appointed unto men once to die" (Hebrews 9:27). James refers to life as a vapor that appears for a little time and then vanishes away (James 4:14). Although Psalms 90:10 gives the average life expectancy as 70 years, Psalms 39:4 comments upon the frailty of man; and 1 Peter 1:24 compares life to withering grass. Regardless of a person's wealth, fame, or position in life, he must face death just like everyone else. "Death is a democracy. It comes to us all and makes all of us equal" (John Gibson). It's wrong to blame God for death. If the blame is placed upon anyone, it should rest upon the shoulders of Adam and Eve, who made the wrong choice many years ago.

Promises in the Scriptures

The words of Job still echo through the centuries to modern times: "If a man die, shall he live again?" (Job

14:14). One only has to turn to the Word of God for full assurance to this question. Even before the resurrection of Christ, a belief in life after death is stated numerous times in the Old Testament. David spoke of this hope in Psalm 16:10,11 and also in 2 Samuel 12:23 when he cried in agony over the death of his infant son: "Can I bring him back again? I shall go to him, but he shall not return to me." Job had this same faith when he said: "And though after my skin worms destroy this body, yet in my flesh shall I see God" (Job 19:26). Isaiah gave hope to the people when he wrote: "Thy dead men shall live, together with my dead body shall they arise" (Isaiah 26:19). Daniel had reference to the resurrection when he said: "And many of them that sleep in the dust of the earth shall awake, some to everlasting life, and some to shame and everlasting contempt" (Daniel 12:2).

The New Testament continues this same line of hope throughout its inspired pages. The book of John speaks of the dead coming from their graves either to a resurrection of life or a resurrection of damnation (5:28,29). Christ encouraged His followers by telling them of a place especially prepared for them (John 14:1-4). The mourners at the house of Jairus laughed scornfully at Jesus when He said: "The damsel is not dead, but sleepeth" (Mark 5:39,40). Personally, I wish that I could have seen the expressions on their faces when our Lord raised her from the dead. Verse 42 is an understatement when it revealed: "And they were astonished with a great astonishment." Christ won the victory over death when He arose from the dead. It is upon this fact that the Christian's hope is based (1 Corinthians 15:12-22). Verse 55 of the same chapter is quoted so often at funerals: "O death, where is thy sting? O grave, where is thy victory?" When Paul wrote to the Thessalonian Christians, he admonished them not to sorrow as those who have no hope but to comfort one another with the teaching of the resurrection (1 Thessalonians 4:13-18). Dr. Elizabeth Kubler-Ross, a noted psychiatrist and expert on reactions to dying, has stated that her research has convinced **her** that life continues beyond the grave.

Instead of the figure of the grim reaper by which death is sometimes portrayed, it is actually a release for something better. Elijah and Job both asked for death (1 Kings 19:4 and Job 7:15). Paul realized the benefits when he said: "For to me to live is Christ, and to die is gain" (Philippians 1:21). Flesh and blood cannot inherit the kingdom of God (1 Corinthians 15:50). How tragic it would be to vegetate throughout all eternity. This fleshly tabernacle must be dissolved before we can enjoy a house not made with hands (2 Corinthians 5:1). Just as we can never know the beauty of the flower until the unattractive, hardened seed is planted in the earth so it may sprout as a plant, neither can a Christian experience the joys of Heaven until his body changes from the physical to the spiritual. A story is told concerning a little girl who claimed as she took an evening walk with her father: "Oh, Daddy, if the wrong side of heaven is so beautiful, what must the right side be!"

The Death Of A Loved One

There is little comfort that can be given when the dying one is not a Christian. There is no pleasant way to face death, either our own or that of a loved one, without Christ. Perhaps the only realistic solace which can be offered is the knowledge that the passing of time tends to lessen the heartbreak resulting from such wounds.

Although there is a certain amount of natural sorrow connected with the passing of a Christian, the outlook is entirely different from the one associated with the death of an unbeliever. It is the death of a Christian that has intrinsic optimistic overtones. In Numbers 23:10 Balaam said: "Let me die the death of the righteous." "Precious in the sight of the Lord is the death of his saints" (Psalms 116:15). Paul felt that whether a Christian lives or dies, he is the Lord's (Romans 14:8). John, who penned such a beautiful description of the joys of Heaven, gave the assurance: "Blessed are the dead which die in the Lord" (Revelation 14:13). Job expressed the right attitude concerning the death of his children when he said: "The Lord gave, and the Lord hath taken away; blessed be the name of the Lord" (Job 1:21).

Even though the Scriptures give immeasurable assurance to the bereaved and although reasoning tells us that the departed one is in a better state, free from suffering, those of us who are left behind are not totally intellectual in our feelings. The reasoning part of the mind usually prevails, but still there is that part down deep inside that does not reason; it reacts as a child who has been hurt and cannot understand. We become so deeply entwined with those we love that when they are taken from us, it seems as if part of our own flesh has been ripped away. Such a wound inevitably will hurt for a time. In fact, it will never completely heal. The bereaved can voice the words of Jonathan as he spoke to David: "Thou shalt be missed, because thy seat will be empty" (1 Samuel 20:18). The seat will always be empty here on this earth because we can never be with that loved one while we live, but we haven't really lost something if we know where it is. We may not be able to touch it, but we know exactly where to find it. Departed Christians act as magnets, drawing us closer to Heaven.

Some years ago I read some very comforting words in which the death of a loved one was compared to a departing sail-boat. We may stand on the shore and watch the boat become smaller and smaller until she is like a speck of white cloud, finally disappearing completely from sight; and we can say, "she's gone." Where has the boat gone? Gone only from our sight. She is still just as real as she was when she left us, but we can no longer see her with our eyes. As we are saying, "She's gone," on the opposite shore others are joyfully shouting, "Here she comes!"

(1) **There are many worries and anxieties connected with the time preceding the death of a loved one.** As the dying one loses his ability to bear his usual responsibilities in the home, they must be assumed by some other member of the family who is usually inept at such tasks. The responsibilities of running a home must be handled by someone when it is the wife and mother who is terminally ill. A dying husband often leaves in the hands of an inexperienced wife many weighty matters which he has shouldered for so long. Quite often there are financial worries, especially in the case of an elderly person who lingers on and on. The problem of loneliness needs to be dealt with realistically. Friends are needed to give sincere companionship and also

to relieve the immediate members of the family for periods of time so the weary ones can have some rest and relaxation.

When a doctor gives his diagnosis of a terminal illness, it is not unnatural for the members of the family to feel anger and even resentment over such a possibility. Once the finality of the diagnosis is accepted, feelings of guilt are common as the family blames itself for failing to see that the dying one did not receive proper medical attention earlier.

The stage immediately preceding death is frequently the most difficult for the survivors to bear. Personalities differ and appropriate action must be taken according to the individual case. Sometimes family members pretend that nothing is wrong and never tell the patient that his case is terminal. To me, this is denying a person a very sacred right - the privilege to prepare himself for death with dignity. Open communication seems the best course. Once the realities have been accepted, it is easier to say, "We know the inevitabilities of the situation. Now what is the best way to use whatever time is left?" Try to make those last days as normal as possible and avoid melancholy scenes. If the patient desires to see fewer people, try to understand that studies have shown this to be his way of gradually detaching himself from this world.

(2) **There are also normal stages following the death of a loved one.** Unfortunately some prolong their grief to an extended period of time and the wound is deliberately kept infected and festered until it finally becomes almost impossible to heal. Their preoccupation with thoughts of the deceased becomes such an obsession that they selfishly withdraw from the mainstream of life to writhe in self-pity. Not only does this indulgence in concern over themselves make their own lives miserable; it also adversely affects those around them.

It is only normal to experience a logical progression of stages after losing someone dear. At first the body automatically protects itself by a sense of initial shock as the mind eases the hurt by allowing the reality to be accepted in small segments. So many details need to be cared for during the first few days. In a sense they can be a blessing because the bereaved is kept busy.

No human has enough inner resources to bear such a burden by himself. When the disciples buried the body of John the Baptist, they "went and told Jesus" (Matthew 14:12). Christ cannot be the comfort He should be in **death** unless he has been a **friend in life.** Our Lord is the first Person to whom we should turn. Next in importance are our Christian friends. Paul admonished all of us to weep with them that weep (Romans 12:15). Space will not permit a detailed discussion, but there are so many ways for friends to say that they care. As the bereaved one, we should allow them to express their concern.

To try to suppress an outward display of grief is very unwise. Various people express their emotions in different ways. A fairly safe course of action would be for us to express as much grief as we honesty **feel** like expressing. God gave us tears for a purpose; they are nature's safety valve. Troubles do not permanently harm us as long as they can flow **through** us, but difficulties arise when they can find no acceptable release and become blocked inside. Then we often pay with psychosomatic illnesses throughout life.

The first few weeks after a death are usually filled with business details and the comfort of visiting friends. After this initial period has passed, the mourner must accept the reality of death, which is usually the most difficult stage. First of all, he must realize that he will never get over the loss. The wounds will gradually heal, but the scar will always remain. The one left behind must learn to say, "Part of me is gone. Where do I go from here?" Most feel some sense of guilt and resentment for failure to do more for the loved one while there were opportunities. This is only natural, for what human being does **everything** he can to make another as happy as possible? Instead of lamenting "If only. . .", we should learn to forgive ourselves and go on from there.

It is best not to be hasty in making important decisions. The reasoning part of the mind is not functioning too clearly at this stage of our lives, and it is difficult to make rational judgments. Rather than give away personal possessions and live to regret such actions or to sell property and then wish we had it back, it is better to defer any permanent decisions until we have returned to normal reasoning. Whether to remain at home or seek a change of scenery depends upon the individual. Some see familiar surroundings as a haven. The wound can heal more quickly for others in a different place.

Creativity resulting from compensating for a loss has been a strong motivating factor behind many great contributions to mankind. Compensations need not be sensational, although some have been so. If our sense of loss causes us to be more understanding and considerate of others, then the world is made a little better by our burden. So often widows and widowers feel like a fifth wheel in social functions. Instead of feeling sorry for ourselves in such a situation, we should find something useful to do and then do it in a cheerful manner. Cheerful people are always needed and desired. If grief is taken in the right way, the mourner can return to the human race as a better, more understanding person.

For a long time there will be good days and bad ones also. If we force ourselves to dwell upon the happy memories and the lessons learned, the good days will outnumber the bad ones. It has been said that time heals. It heals **if** it is used properly. The melody that the loved one played on the instrument of our hearts will never be played again, but there is no reason to cover the keyboard and never use it as a source of comfort and encouragement to others.

I am thankful that I cannot speak from experience; but, to me, one of the most diffcult losses to suffer would be that of a child. I have a friend who has suffered great physical pain and   discomfort in a triumphant manner. I mentioned this in a card to her one day and received the following reply regarding her patience.

We lost our little boy at the age of four (the only child we had at that time). Of course our hearts were broken. We sat down to talk things over after the funeral and agreed that we could never forget, but at the same time we must not remember with anger, bitterness, discouragement or vain regret. We simply did the best we could at the time and left the issue in God's hands, for He makes no mistakes. I think I learned then to have more patience, faith, trust and hope I can continue to feel that way.

Edgar A. Guest wrote so beautifully:

"I'll lend you for a little while
  A child of mine," God said,
"For you to have the while he lives,
  And mourn for when he's dead.

It may be six or seven years
  Or twenty-two or three;
But will you 'till I call him back
  Take care of him for me?

He'll bring his charms to gladden you
  And, should his stay be brief,
You'll have his lovely memories
  As a solace for your grief.

I cannot promise he will stay,
  Since all from earth return;
But there are lessons taught below
  I want this child to learn.

I've looked the whole world over
  In search for teachers true;
And from the throngs that crowd life's land,
  I have chosen you.

Now, will you give him all your love
  Nor think the labor vain?
Nor hate me when I come to take
  This lent child back again?"

I fancied that I heard them say:
  "Dear Lord, Thy will be done.
For all the joys Thy child will bring
  The risk of grief we'll run.

We'll shelter him with tenderness,
  We'll love him while we may.
And for the happiness we've known
  Forever grateful stay.

But should Thy angel call for him
  Much sooner than we've planned,
We'll brave the bitter grief that comes
  And try to understand."

As it is true in nature, so is it also true in the lives of humans. There are shadows, many of them; but the shadows are caused by real objects. We could eliminate the shadows by never having the objects in the first place. We could prevent many of the shadows of our lives by never knowing or loving the persons whose absence causes those shadows. If we are to miss the heartaches, we must also forfeit the love and pleasure which those dear ones have given to us while they lived. We cannot have one without the other.

Suggestions for Class Use
Lesson Twelve

1. Use these Scriptures to discuss the brevity of life: Ecclesiastes 3:1,2; Hebrews 9:27; James 4:14; Psalms 90:10; Psalms 39:4; and 1 Peter 1:24.
2. What instances in the Old Testament indicate that there was hope for life after death even then?
3. Cite New Testament passages that give full assurance of life after death.
4. Why did Paul feel that for him "to live is Christ, and to die is gain?" (See Philippians 1:21.)
5. How can a person deal with the death of a loved one who is not a Christian?
6. Use these passages to establish the fact that the death of a Christian is an occasion for thankfulness, not sorrow: Numbers 23:10; Psalms 116:15; Romans 14:8; Revelation 14:13; Job 1:21.
7. Before class time assign a member the sketching of the illustration concerning the comparison of death to a sail-boat and then explain it to the class.
8. What are some of the worries and additional strains placed upon families when they learn that one member is terminally ill?

9. Do you feel that impending death should be discussed openly with the victim or kept from him? State your reasons.

10. Why do the bereaved frequently experience a state of shock at the time of death? Is this good or bad?

11. To whom should we logically turn during a time of bereavement?

12. What are the advantages of an outward expression of grief? Should such feelings be repressed?

13. Assign a class member the task of doing additional research concerning the mourning customs of the Jews.

14. How much should children be told about death?

15. Do we ever completely get over the death of a loved one? Would we really want to do so?

16. Why is it best not to make hasty permanent decisions? Probably the class members can share some personal mistakes they have made.

17. How can compensation for the loss of a loved one be the motivating factor for great accomplishments?

18. From the class glean successful ways to deal with the death of a child. You might like to ask the members to obtain advice from their friends who have faced this problem.

19. Sorrow is caused by the loss of something very dear to us. Would any of us want to spare ourselves that sorrow by refusing to open our hearts to love?

13

The Cup of Death - Our Own

"Father, I can intellectually face dying; and yet there is a part of me that cringes over the prospect. There were so many things I had hoped to accomplish in my lifetime. Why do I have to leave my family and work now? Please, Lord, give me the strength to face this last remaining hurdle with dignity as a child of the King."

Every time the clock ticks one more second, someone in this world dies. As Benjamin Franklin wrote, "Death takes no bribes." It is coming to each of us. Even though a discussion of the subject may make us feel uncomfortable, all of us must face **this** problem sooner or later. Planting in our minds at this time the seeds of what a Christian's reaction should be will help us accept death with grace whenever it comes our way.

Life is so fragile. A person can be in perfect health with everything in his favor and yet be dead within the next minute. We can all echo the words of David as he spoke to Jonathan: "Truly, as the Lord liveth, and thy soul liveth, there is but a step between me and death" (1 Samuel 20:3).

God placed us here on this earth to give us an opportunity to prepare ourselves for eternity and take others with us. Our life span may seem very important and lengthy; but, compared with the history of mankind, our few years spent in this body are similar to a tiny dot on a line many miles long. The question under consideration is not the **duration** of our lives but what we accomplish while we're here. How much will we be missed? When we continue living in the hearts of those left behind, have we really passed out of existence? "When a man dies he clutches in his hands only that which he has given away in his lifetime" (Rousseau). It's a simple lesson but one that is sometimes difficult to learn.

Acceptance

Most of us can be quite philosophical about death in general, but our own death is a different matter. At that time it is not easy to take our own advice. For a Christian, the ultimate in victory is not just to accept the deaths of the masses but also his own with dignity.

A number of scientific studies have been made concerning the reactions of terminally ill patients. Most of them seem to follow a fairly predictable pattern. When a person first learns that his illness is fatal, his initial reaction is one of denial. To deny that death is imminently probable gives the body and senses the shielding effects of shock and allows time for the truth to be accepted. This is usually a temporary stage which soon is replaced by one of anger and resentment as the patient reasons that others go on living. Why does his time have to be cut short? After he passes through this reaction, he frequently tries to beg for an extension of life by promising to do some things which he has previously failed to accomplish. Sometimes these phases overlap, but depression generally follows the bargaining process. As the body weakens and is in pain, it is most difficult to maintain a cheerful outlook. The terminally ill patient worries about the financial strain which he is placing on his family. Often there is a sense of guilt and certainly a natural sorrow over leaving loved ones behind. Doctors recommend that members of the family refrain from a false sense of cheerfulness and an attitude that everything is going to be all right. The sick one must be given the realistic support and love to work out his own solutions to what is inevitable. Some may never reach the final stage of acceptance, but those who do so have won a victory. Acceptance is not a giddy, light-hearted gaiety. It is not happiness in the usual sense of the word but is instead a victory over the dread of death. There is a vast difference in acceptance and resignation. The latter implies defeat, a hopeless giving up. Even though one accepts his death, there normally remains a faint shred of hope. When this hope is lost, death is usually imminent.

We've examined the findings of medical science. Now let's turn our thoughts to spiritual acceptance. A Christian, of all people, should know what he wants out of life and also how he will face death when the time comes. Such a bulwark of strength is impossible without the proper foundation. Slowly but surely, as one year rolls into another, a Christian's trust in God increases. As we mature in the faith, we realize that we can never be good enough to merit our salvation. By faith we accept God's conditions by doing our part and God's grace spans the gap. If perfection were necessary for entrance into Heaven, none of us would ever make it. Day by day we make mistakes and fall short, **but** we sincerely repent of our faults as we commit them and try again. Thus, without a sense of piety or perfection, we can know that salvation is ours because we believe God's promises to be true. Usually it's a fairly simple matter to predict how a child of God will react to death; he faces death in the same manner as he faces life. We can't answer the call of death affirmatively unless we've also said yes to life.

After The Verdict, Then What?

A Christian who knows that death is imminent usually becomes more conscious of small blessings that perhaps he never noticed before. The awareness gives a new depth and beauty of life and truly makes each day a special one - a tiny capsule of time, complete in itself. No one knows that tomorrow will be his. All that any of us can realistically hope for is today, and we may not have all of that. Accept each new day-for what it is - a gift from God. Use it wisely and then that night lay it back at God's feet as your offering to Him. The acceptance of death is easier for any of us if we can only learn to live one day at a time.

The terminally ill patient will probably outlive some of his friends and acquaintances who seem quite healthy. Accidents and diseases take their toll on those who least suspect them. When my life was hanging in the balance for a number of weeks, I had the support of so many friends by cards, prayers, and thoughtful deeds. While writing the material for this chapter, I stopped and thought of those who were seemingly so healthy at that time but whom I have outlived. Even the neurosurgeon who examined me for possible brain damage shortly after my accident only lived for a few months. The whole point is this: the terminally ill person has not had a curse placed upon him. He will probably outlive many who have no present thoughts of death. One day at a time is all that **any** of us can hope for. Live each day to the fullest and leave the rest to God. In John 7:33 Christ said: "Yet a little while am I with you, and then I go unto him that sent me." The knowledge that death would soon be a reality did not change our Lord's style of living. He continued as He had in the past - teaching, rebuking, performing miracles, and going about His daily routine.

Death with Dignity

Many articles have recently appeared throughout the news media concerning the right of an individual to die with dignity. When there is no hope, how long should the patient be kept alive through artificial measures? A number of people have signed a Living Will, in which they have requested that they be allowed to die naturally when there is no reasonable expectation of recovery. Modern medical science has solved many problems, but it has also created this one.

When the time comes that we can say with Job: "The graves are ready for me" (Job 17:1), we should have matured enough to have a personal faith, not just a theory, and make the final step in our lives the most victorious one of all. For this trip the luggage must be packed and sent on ahead.

So live that when thy summons comes to join
The innumberable caravan which moves
To that mysterious realm, where each shall take
His chamber in the silent halls of death,
Thou go not, like the quarry-slave at night,
Scourged to his dungeon, but, sustained and soothed
By an unfaltering trust, approach thy grave

Like one who wraps the drapery of his couch
About him, and lies down to pleasant dreams.
                                    William Cullen Bryant

While we as Christians should approach death with
dignity, there should be no sense of shame in feeling a
certain amount of apprehension in traveling an unknown
path. At that time we are in somewhat the same
predicament as the children of Israel when they were
getting ready to cross over the Jordan: "Ye have not passed
this way heretofore" (Joshua 3:4). Abraham started on his
journey to the land of Canaan in faith for "he went out, not
knowing whither he went" (Hebrews 11:8). Someone has
wisely said that faith builds a bridge across the gulf of
death.

"It is not in man that walketh to direct his steps"
(Jeremiah 10:23), but we do have a Supreme Example in
whose steps we can follow (1 Peter 2:21). Christ was divine
and yet He lived in a human body and experienced human
emotions as He agonized over an impending, cruel death.
"His sweat was as it were great drops of blood falling down
to the ground" (Luke 22:44). Courage is not the absence of
fear; it is going ahead in spite of natural anxieties.

Death is a valley through which we must travel with only
one companion. "Yea, though I walk through the valley of
the shadow of death, I will fear no evil: for **thou** art with
me" (Psalms 23:4). As we travel this narrow, unknown path
between the present and eternity, we do exactly as the
psalmist says. We **walk**. We do not blithefully skip through.
Neither do we run. Instead, we slowly plod, placing one foot
in front of the other as we cautiously feel our way along; but
we are **going** somewhere. We are never alone, for He is
always there, saying, in effect: "My child, I know the way is
dark and foreboding; but do not fear. I have traveled along
the same path and I will help you." William Jennings Bryan
very beautifully described the valley of death when he said,
"Christ has made of death a narrow, starlit strip between
the companionships of yesterday and the reunions of
tomorrow."

Death is the veil which those who live call life.
They sleep, and it is lifted.

Percy Bysshe Shelley

It is fairly easy to give advice, but such words are more
meaningful when they come from one who has triumphantly
achieved. Several years ago a letter appeared in a
Chattanooga church bulletin. It was written to a Christian
who was dying because of a maligant brain tumor by a
woman who had victoriously conquered a similar problem.
Her words were so encouraging that I would like to share
some of them with you.

"There is a destiny - that makes us brothers. None goes
his way alone! All that we put into the lives of others,
comes back into your own." You have given much - please
accept what I offer!

I am a stranger to you - except that I am your sister in
Christ, and for that reason I have compassion for you at
this time - for I, in part, know some of what you are going
through, for I too, have cancer.

We have much in common. Both at the peak of life, having
raised our families, solved many problems (I assume) and
now it seemed that there were many wonderful years
ahead to make many dreams come true. . .and in only one
day - it seemed that the dreams shattered as the doctors
gave the verdicts - as they saw them.

I had breast surgery five years ago - and only six months
ago was told that I had a complete recovery - only to have
it reappear three months ago. I cannot take additional
radiation - and now my life is in the hands of God - and
experiments of science.

I remember well the day I heard the news - and the
numbness that I felt - and those days that passed as I
fought and prayed that God would give me the strength
and the courage to ACCEPT my fate.

My prayers have been answered - as I pray yours will be - and now I am "Out of the fog that surrounded me" and there is peace in my heart.

Fear and imagination can do much to harm a person. I decided to replace fear with FAITH. I know that all that any of us have is only one MINUTE, one HOUR, and one DAY at a time. All of a sudden I was trying to face months or years ahead instead of just taking it a minute at a time. . .for I know that any one can take, with God's help, just little minute at a time. . .or a second.

I am enjoying my days. My spirit is being strengthened each day. I find that I have a new dimension to help other people and I know that much good will come into other lives because of my own struggle.

You and I have spent almost a life time - getting ready for what we now face - and our acceptance in the time we have left can mean more, in influence, than perhaps all of the words we have ever uttered.

Something good comes from adversity. . .and if my understanding of what you have been going through. and the feeble words that I have tried to utter - can in any small way help you, then I will count it as being worth my having to walk in the valley too!

May God grant you the courage to accept what you cannot change - and to find happiness in each passing day.

I am one of the more fortunate ones. In 1970 I stared death in the face for a number of weeks; and, according to medical expectations, I should have died. But I didn't. I have no way of knowing how long it will be until I face the same situation again, but someday I will. I have walked far enough into that valley to know that I will never have to face **any** problem alone. I suppose we have to learn how to die before we can truly know how to live.

Suggestions for Class Use
Lesson Thirteen

1. Why is it wise to plan for death, especially our own, before the time actually comes? Is this being morbid or realistic?
2. Why were we placed here on this earth? What is the only important consideration?
3. Why is our own personal death so much harder to cope with than death in general?
4. Studies have been made concerning the stages through which a terminally ill patient passes. Discuss each of them. Do you agree or disagree? State your reasons.
5. What is the difference in acceptance of death and resignation?
6. How can a Christian build the proper foundation for the acceptance of his own death?
7. How can humans, who are so frail and make so many mistakes, have an assurance of their salvation? Is it wrong to say that we know what our eternal destiny will be?
8. "A child of God faces death in the same manner that he faces life." Do you agree or disagree?
9. How can living only one day at a time enable a Christian to withstand the pressures of an impending death?
10. Did our Lord make any changes in His style of living when He knew that death was imminent?
11. Select a panel to discuss the advantages and disadvantages of artificially extending life when there is no reasonable hope of recovery.
12. Describe what death with dignity involves.
13. A certain amount of apprehension is only natural when each of us reaches an unfamiliar path. Is this a cause of shame or a display of lack of faith? Discuss.
14. How did Christ face death in the garden?
15. As near and dear as our friends and loved ones have been to us, when we actually reach the brink of death, we must make the remainder of the journey without them. Who walks through the final valley with us?

Read Psalms 23 slowly and allow the true meaning to penetrate the hearts of the class members.
16. Read the letter quoted in the lesson aloud in class and comment.

CONCLUSION

I'd like to close our study with an allegory that comes from a heart that has learned to trust.

Once a child of the Master gleefully set about the task of weaving on a very large loom as his fumblng fingers learned to manipulate each thread handed him by the Master Weaver.

"This is really no trouble at all," the youngster thought as he viewed the pleasant, sunny fabric he was weaving. Then the Master Weaver handed the child his first dark thread. "What am I to do with this?" the novice asked. "I thought the Master's children were given only threads of the bright, sunny colors. This dark thread will ruin the cloth."

"You do not understand now, my child; but the dark thread is necessary. See what you can do with it."

Fumbling in anger and resentment over his assignment, the apprentice clumsily made an attempt to weave the dark color in and out among the light hues. The work was far from perfect, but the Master gave only encouragement. "That's fine, my child. You are learning. I merely ask that you try."

The next threads offered the young weaver were of his favorite bright color and he heaved a sigh of relief that his dark thread was behind him. As he worked confidently with the brightly colored threads, the Master tapped him on the shoulder and gave him another dark thread of a different hue. "But Master, I have just finished using a dark one. Why am I given another?"

"You may not understand, my little one; but I know best. See how well you can manage this one."

Having already dealt with one dark thread, the child

knew all the frustrations involved, but he loved his Master and believed that He knew best so the young one tried once more. Even **he** knew that his work was far from perfect, but the Master seemed pleased over his efforts so he put his heart into the task.

As the days lengthened into years, the young child, who had now become a stooped, hoary-headed old man, slowly came to expect the dark threads to be given him from time to time along with the bright ones; and his resentment lessened. Weaving them into the cloth became a challenge. He was so far removed from his first efforts that no longer could he even remember what they were like, and he was too close to his present work to have any sort of perspective of the over-all picture.

After many years of tears, frustrations, and heartbreak, the broken old man was called by the Master to cease his labors and come rest with Him on a quiet, grassy hillside overlooking the valley where so many years had been spent at the loom.

"Faithful one, I have witnessed your heartbreak and frustration all these years with tears in My eyes, for I once was given a loom similar to yours upon which to weave. I, too, experienced sorrows and frustrations. But no one can enter my Father's house until he has mastered the art of weaving the daily threads on the loom of his life. I could see your mistakes, but I knew that you would learn if only you did not lose faith in Me and would keep on trying. I, too, had to learn to weave similar dark threads into my cloth; and I know how difficult they were to manage. Now that you can view your work from a distance, look at the loom upon which you have been weaving all these years."

As the broken form lifted his head to gaze upon the panoramic scene, he could scarcely believe his eyes. There were his first awkward attempts at using the dark threads. As his eyesight progressed from beginning to end, he was amazed at the beauty and perspective which the dark threads had given to his cloth and how much more skillfully his pattern was woven as it neared the end.

"Now you can see what the dark threads have meant to your tapestry. Without them your cloth would have had no depth. Aren't you glad you had enough faith in Me to continue trying? Your years of weaving brought tears, frustrations, and disappointments. You stayed with the task, never fully understanding the importance of those dark threads but trusting Me as I gave them to you. Now all your hard work is behind. My Father has prepared a wonderful place for you to live throughout eternity. Because you have remained faithful, there will be no more sorrow nor pain. My Father will wipe all tears from your eyes. Now your stooped back will be straightened. All things will be made new."

As Isaiah had prophesied: ". . .he shall gather the lambs with his arm, and carry them in his bosom. . ." (Isaiah 40:11), the Master Weaver tenderly gathered into His arms the frail, pain-ridden body of this child who had now grown old and entered the gates that would never close, a place more wonderful than any human could possibly imagine. Never again would there be the arduous task of weaving. There would be no more sorrow nor pain. Neither would there be any more dark threads. There would only be eternal basking in the light of the Father's presence.

But the loom with the tapestry was left in the valley with numerous other looms, including the perfect one of the Master Weaver. Many had been abandoned after a few unsuccessful tries, but some beautiful tapestries remained as citadels of encouragement to other beginners that the task **could** be done if only they trusted the Master Weaver and faithfully kept on trying.

"He that overcometh shall inherit
all things, and I will be his God,
and he shall be my son."

"And God himself shall be with them,
and be their God. And God shall wipe
away all tears from their eyes; and
there shall be no more death, neither
sorrow, nor crying, neither shall
there be any more pain: for the
former things are passed away."